Kathleen Dayus was born in Hockley, Birmingham in 1903. She still lives in Birmingham and was awarded an honorary Master of Arts degree by the University of Birmingham in December 1992 in recognition of her contribution to the writing of Birmingham's history.

Also by Kathleen Dayus

Her People
Where There's Life
All My Days
The Best of Times

THE

GHOSTS

of

YESTERYEAR

Kathleen Dayus

Virago Press
An Imprint of
Little, Brown and Company (U.K.)
Brettenham House
Lancaster Place
London WC2E 7EN

A *Virago* Book

Published by Virago Press 2000

Copyright © Kathleen Dayus 2000

The moral right of the author has been asserted

A CIP catalogue record for this book is
available from the British Library

ISBN 1 86049 808 6

Typeset in Cochin by M Rules
Printed and bound in Great Britain by
M̶ ̶l̶ ̶ ̶ ̶f̶ ̶C̶h̶-̶t̶h̶-̶m̶ ̶p̶l̶c̶.̶ ̶Chatham, Kent

These stories of my life, and those of my children whilst in those dreaded homes, are told in my autobiographies, published by Virago Press, London. Now I live alone, my children happily married with several grandchildren whom I will always love and cherish. But I shall never forget those turbulent years.

I am now beginning to write about life as it happens now, from day to day, and I pray the Good Lord will spare me the time to finish. 'Before it's too late,' as my grandma Hannah used to say.

KATHLEEN DAYUS

Contents

Early Days

A few years ago I went to town to buy Christmas presents. As I wandered along Constitution Hill and Great Hampton Street, I found myself in the Hockley district, now famously known as the Jewellery Quarter. This was a district I remembered well from those many long years ago. As I walked along, the memories returning, I began to feel sad and alone as I recalled this place in which I was born, when the district was a hive of humanity where overcrowded families of many generations tried to exist. These were once 'my people' of my generation.

As I passed the iron gates of the cemetery, I thought to go and look at some graves. I knew it was no use looking for the graves of my family and friends, or the neighbours whose little children I once went to school with. Their burial places were the communal graves marked only by mounds of earth, created after Hitler dropped his bombs without warning in April 1941.

After leaving the cemetery, I walked along Frederick Street to Albion Street. On the corner of Legge Lane stood the old derelict fire station and stable yards where the firemen kept their wagons and horses. There were once living quarters above the stables, but now, sad to say, these premises are used by several businesses. I began to think of those happy times many years ago, when as children we would sit on the wall near the stables and watch the firemen slide down a brass pole. Each night we would watch them bring out their horses and harness them to the wagons ready for the six o'clock practice. Often we could be seen on the opposite side of the street, trying to keep pace with the horses. Off they would gallop as the big brass bell clanged and they drove around the square and back, rolling the rubber hoses along the pavement after them. Opposite the old fire station is the George and Dragon, which has also had a face lift and is now frequented by business people working in the Jewellery Quarter.

I remembered the pub near our house, where my brother, sister and I sang carols for halfpennies or a penny to buy sugar mice or a chocolate Father Christmas to hang on our home-made Christmas tree. Sometimes we would run errands for our neighbours for farthings so we could buy crêpe paper to make coloured chains to stretch across the room and hang across picture frames. If a neighbour hadn't a copper to spare they would give us a piece of bread pudding, and glad of this we were as we were always hungry. Sometimes we would stand outside Gillotts pen factory and beg for food as workers came out of the big gates at night.

A short distance from the George and Dragon stood our small church school. It had also been bombed twice during the War and lay derelict for many years, well after this district had been rebuilt. Now all that can be seen is the remainder of the tower, where once the iron bell used to clang, to remind us kids it was time to be inside school; when it stopped you would be locked out until two o'clock.

The Georgian church school was ruled by the old eccentric vicar, Canon Smith, from our local church, St Pauls.

As I stood looking down from the top of Camden Grove at the ruins of our playground, I thought of the many times my brother Frankie, my sister Liza and myself, with many other ragged and hungry children, fled up that cobbled alleyway before that school bell stopped ringing.

One Monday morning, we three were flying up the hill when all of a sudden we heard the last clang of the bell. We were too late and the heavy oak door closed against us. We knew we would be punished and began to weep. We'd missed our breakfast of bread and jam and an enamel mug of hot cocoa. And when Mum found out, we not only had the cane before we went back to school at two o'clock, but when we got to school our teacher was waiting with *his* cane at the ready. We were scared, too, when it was time for Vicar Smith to arrive and give us his lecture. After that we learnt never to be late again.

I was four years of age and a very inquisitive child when I first began to notice the hardships and poverty my parents and neighbours had to endure, not forgetting the many family quarrels as tempers flared when things didn't go right.

Families of all ages tried to earn a living and bring in a few coppers. Often we would have to help our mother by carding linen buttons or hooks and eyes, or chopping and selling firewood from door to door. I would see my mother and neighbours washing in the brewhouse by candle light, hoping to get something washed and hung to dry around the room, ready for the pawn shop the next day. We had a smack if we didn't duck under the wet clothes. Many children like myself had to help with these chores far into the night; it was no wonder we had the cane for falling asleep in school.

That was the *old* Jewellery Quarter, where they made pearl buttons, buckles and cheap brass jewellery, and where wages were low. Today this district is a thriving industry, with makers of expensive gold and silver jewellery.

My mother never seemed to find time to explain or provide answers to things we wished to know about life and love; it was no wonder we six children, three girls and three boys, grew up in ignorance for many years. Often I would hear her bawl when tempers frayed, 'I ain't got time to bother with the questions! Get out from under my bloody feet and do summat useful!' Other times, 'I wish we could all clear out of this godforsaken bloody rat hole, 'tain't even big enough to swing a cat round, let alone tryin' ter raise a family!'

How well I still remember those broken down old houses for miles around, where rats and mice bred everywhere. Many people had two, three or even four cats, but they never seemed to get rid of the rats. I believe the cats were afraid of them.

There was no work for thousands and no repairs done by the landlords, yet governments always found money for wars. Therefore it was not until Hitler decided *he* didn't like these old condemned buildings either and destroyed them with bombs, killing and maiming thousands young and old during the Second World War, that any changes were made. Those left standing were still occupied by families, but some were lucky enough to be rehoused in prefabs made from sheets of corrugated iron and concrete by 1960.

How We Got a New Door

Our was not a happy home. There were too many quarrels over money or where the next meal would come from, and voices would be raised until Mum had the last word. My mother was a very hard woman with a temper to match, always quarrelling with the neighbours when she couldn't get her own way.

Never at any time in my childhood can I remember her loving me or giving me a kiss and a cuddle, and I missed this very much when I saw other mothers kiss their children on the way to school. Often I tried to please her, but she never seemed to have time for me, or even to listen, although I was always at her beck and call when she needed me. 'Katie! Fetch me this!' 'Katie, do that!' Even before I'd finished one job, it was: 'Leave that, yer can do that later! Do this!'

I was always given the dirtiest jobs, yet I never dared to refuse. One of the jobs allocated to me was fetching the slop bucket from beside my parents' bed and taking it out to the yard, to be emptied down the dry closet. It was a wonder my lungs didn't burst the way I held my nose and breath. After rinsing the bucket under the tap in the yard my mother would always inspect if before I took it back upstairs.

I shall never forget the first time I did this job. As soon as she inspected it she caught hold of my hair and bawled in my ear: 'Yer can tek it back and do it proper or I'll tip it on yer bloody 'ead!' After that, I always gave the bucket an extra scrub before placing it back in their bedroom. I did more than my share of dirty jobs, just to please her, but it made no difference.

My young brother and I were the only two in the family that understood each other. Often we sat on the wooden sofa and he would say things to make me laugh. One day when we thought Mum was upstairs, I told him about the slop bucket.

'Yes, I know,' he replied.

'Who told yer?'

'Mum's pet! Her sitting on Gran's rocker – Liza,' he replied, pointing at her. 'An' yer know, Katie, we'd have many a laugh if that slop bucket could talk.' He smiled.

Suddenly Mum seemed to spring from nowhere and as she gave Frankie and me a couple of back-handers she yelled out, 'Yer can both laugh them off! Now get up off yer bloody arses an' do summat useful!'

There was always a smug look on Liza's face when she saw us being punished.

Jobs around the house were to be shared between the three of us, but my sister Liza was Mum's favourite and

she got away with many an excuse. I couldn't understand why Mum didn't see through her. She'd whimper,
'Mum, I got earache,' or, 'I've got pains in me belly,' or
some such excuse to get out of doing her share of chores.
Once I saw her spit on her fingers and rub it into her
eyes.

I tried to squeeze a few tears too, but it never turned
out right for me. I was only pushed away and felt the flat
of Mum's hand. I never knew until I was told many years
later that I was an unwanted child.

The only three people that I ever really loved were
my dad, my granny and my brother Frank. My dad was
a well-built man, with dark hair and a rounded bald
patch on the top of his head. He also had kind blue eyes
which often twinkled when he smiled, his aquiline nose
and his teeth were perfect, and he had a good sense of
humour.

Often when my mother was out shopping with Liza,
he would make us sit on the pegged rug in front of the
fire and read to us from the *War Cry* or recite the comic
bits from *Punch*. I looked forward to those happy times.
As I did when he taught me to read and write when I
was only four years old. He often corrected me if I spelt
or pronounced a word wrongly; I would have to repeat it
again and again until I got it off by heart.

I remember Mum's harsh words when Dad tried to
teach Liza. 'She'll learn quick enough at school,' she
would say.

'She knows sod all!' I once heard Dad reply angrily.
'An' another thing. I don't want any of our kids growing
up illiterate!'

Suddenly Mum put her hands on her hips and glared at him. 'Yer mean me, don't yer?' she exclaimed. 'It warn't my fault I carn't read and write. I 'ad no schoolin'. I 'ad ter tek care of me brothers and sisters an' I never 'ad a father neither!'

'I've heard all that before, Polly, no reason to shout!' he replied. As he went to put his arm around her she shouted as she pushed him away: 'Leave me alone!'

'Polly! Will you listen to reason? I've offered to teach you many times, but you're only interested when I read the *News of the World* to you. It's not too late. Now sit down and listen to what I'm going to say!'

'It's too late for me!' she cried out impatiently. 'I ain't got the time anyway. I've got me washin' ter 'ang out afower it rains.'

'Never mind the washing. This is more important. For the last time, will you let me try to teach yer?'

''Ow many times do I 'ave ter say, it's too late!' Mum exclaimed.

'It's never too late! We can always find time for at least an hour at night, after the kids have gone to bed.'

'No, Sam. It's a waste of time. Any'ow I've got too much ter do.'

I could see that Dad was now losing his patience. I heard him say, 'Well, have it your own way, Polly. But remember this, I am never going shopping with you agen!'

'Why? What 'ave I done now?' she demanded.

'Well, if you want to know why, I feel shamed and embarrassed. When I check up the groceries, suddenly you stick your fingers up in the air and count 'em in front of all the customers,' he replied as he stormed out of the house, banging the door behind him.

A few days before I was five, I had to be registered at the church school at the top of the hill. There were more arguments.

'She's got to go ter school,' I heard my dad say.

'But she ain't ready. Any'ow, she's gotta 'elp around the 'ouse.'

'You'll do as I say, Polly, and no more excuses!'

'But I don't 'avta tek 'er till next week!' Mum replied.

'Well! See that yer do. I don't want another summons, I ain't paid the last one yet.'

'Wot one's that?' Mum cried as she glared at him.

'Yer know very well the one, the half-crown for the chimney being on fire. Now don't let's have any more arguments. And another thing, we'll have to get swept agen.'

'The sweep said 'e warn't paid for the last one.'

'Well, here's two shillings and don't forget me change. I'll be in the George tonight and I'll ask if you've paid him.' Dad threw the two-shilling piece across the table and hurried out of the house, slamming the door behind him.

Every time anyone slammed the door I expected it to fall off its hinges and wondered how long it would last. I didn't have to wait much longer.

Two nights later there was a terrible storm of hail, rain, snow and howling winds, which shook the whole foundation. 'It's a terrible night, Polly. I never known a storm like it,' I heard Dad say as they both sat by the fire.

I was huddled with Frankie and Liza on the wooden sofa beneath the window when suddenly we heard a loud clap of thunder. It shook the window frames, and as we heard the glass break, Mum yelled, 'Yo three better drag that sofa away from the winda an' bring it up ter the fire!'

As Dad began to move the fireguard and steel fender to make room for us, he asked if there was any more coal down the cellar. 'No, Sam, that's the last,' Mum replied.

'Shall I go down?' Frankie asked. 'P'raps I can scrape enough slack or rubbish ter keep the fire going.'

Soon he was back with a couple of mouldy old boots, a wooden clog and some slack in the tin bowl. As he handed the bowl over to Dad, Mum helped to pack the boots and clog with stewed tea leaves and wet slack. These were put in the hearth ready to bank up the fire for the night.

We all sat around the fire to keep warm. Mum said, 'I 'ope that'll last till the coalman comes termorra, Sam. That's if we're still 'ere.'

'Don't be so bloody morbid, woman. Of course we'll be here. Anyway, it seems ter be easing off now.'

'Thank God,' she replied, just as there was another loud clash of thunder with fork and sheet lightning. To make matters worse, the paraffin lamp decided it had had enough too. Now we only had the firelight to see by.

'Ain't there any more paraffin, Polly?' Dad asked.

'No. I emptied the can early on. Any'ow, Katie can get them pieces of candles outa the drawer, and mind yer don't knock anythink over!' she added.

After they were lit, Dad told us to take his old Army coat off the door and get ourselves up to bed. 'You'll be warmer up there. Me and yer mum will be up later,' he said as he began to bank up the fire with the rubbish.

As Frankie got the coat off the door, the window frame shook again and we heard slates fall off the roof. As soon as we had wished our parents 'good night' Mum yelled out, 'What's bloody good about it?'

'Now, now, Polly, we'll have to make the best of it, till morning, then we'll be able ter see what damage it's done. Now I'd better bolt the back door and we'll have an early night.'

'Dad!' I cried out as I got halfway up the stairs, worried about my elder brother. 'Don't bolt the door! Jack ain't come home yet and he might be on his way now.'

'It's all right, love. Jack ain't no fool ter be out on a night like this. He's very likely still at his mates playing cards.'

'Or playin' with 'is fancy woman,' Mum exclaimed. Dad didn't reply other than to tell me to hurry to bed before the candle burnt itself out.

As soon as we entered the attic we began to shiver; we took off only our boots and jumped into bed fully clothed. That night the three of us huddled together to keep warm. After pulling the grey blanket and coats over us, Frankie and Liza soon fell asleep, but I lay awake a long time, listening to the howling winds and praying that the good Lord would keep us all safe. Soon after, I closed my eyes and fell asleep.

I don't know how long I slept, but I was wide awake again as I felt our cat snuggle beneath me. I began to wonder what would happen to our home if the storm kept raging. I knew we didn't have much as regards furniture. There was a wooden, well worn, scrubbed square table in the centre of the room, one ladderback chair, two backless chairs, a rickety old wooden sofa, a three-legged stool, an orange box and my grandma's rocking chair. On the lime-washed walls were odd photos of some of my sisters and brothers who had died before I was born.

A pegged rag rug lay on the hearth and helped to hide the broken slabs. There was a recess each side of the fireplace. In one, our old wooden mangle stood behind the stairs door; in the other was a shallow, dark brown earthenware sink, but we never had running water or a tap. When we needed water it was fetched from a stand pipe at the bottom of the yards, where neighbours would queue on wash days. Often I would hear strong language when the water pipe was frozen.

I was awakened the second time by raindrops falling on my face. As I opened my eyes and looked up, I saw a gaping hole in the ceiling and rain running along the rafters. Quickly I jumped out of bed and almost dragged my brother and sister with me as I screamed, 'Wake up! Wake up, you two!' As soon as he saw what was happening Frankie joined me, but we had to pull Liza out before she would move, and as Frankie and I tried to drag the iron bedsteads to another part of the room, we heard Dad call up the stairs, 'What's going on up there! Yer know it's the middle of the night!' As we tried to explain, Dad came bounding up the stairs to help. When he saw what had happened he said there was nothing to be done until daybreak, but to follow him and bring the blanket and overcoats.

As soon as we entered their bedroom, Mum started to rave and shout. 'I ain't 'avin' 'em sleepin' with us! It ain't decent, Sam!'

'It ain't their fault they've been rained on! Anyway, they'll have ter sleep with us until the roof is mended. Now, you three,' he added, 'don't stand there shivering. Jump in. There's plenty of room when yer mum decides ter move over.'

Still fully clothed we climbed in, and after a while I noticed Mum calm down and begin to smile as she turned to face Dad and snuggled up to him. I often wonder what he whispered to make her smile. The rest of the night we all huddled in the bed together. And that was the first time I can ever remember sleeping with my mum and dad.

Next morning, as we awoke, the sun was shining but it was still very cold. All at once Mum yelled as she tried to push us out of bed, 'Come on yo three. Get up an' 'elp yer dad!'

'They'd better stay where they are – and you, Polly – while I go and rake the fire up and bring yer up a jug of hot cocoa.'

My brother and I smiled and winked at each other as Dad slipped on his trousers and hurried down the stairs. We suddenly heard him cry out, 'Oh my God! Polly! Polly! Yer better come down here, the place is flooded!' Barefoot we ran down the stairs, Mum following behind. When we got there we couldn't believe our eyes. There

was black muddy water to a depth of six inches everywhere we looked. This had been caused by the gales and
heavy rain coming down the chimney and bringing loads
of soot with them. All the chattels we owned were float-
ing, along with the front door. We could now see other
neighbours sweeping out their rooms too. After the scare
and Mum's swearing and aggravation, we set to at once
with the bass broom and the house broom, while dad
tried to salvage what he could.

Neighbours from houses at the top of the hill came to
help with hot drinks and cast-off clothes and old boots,
which we were very grateful for. Two days it took for
almost everything to dry out and get back to normal –
except the door. When Dad tried to keep it up with
Mum's washing line prop, the prop snapped in two.
When he saw the angry look on Mum's face he began to
smile.

'Nothin' ter smile about!' she cried out.

'Oh well, Polly,' he replied. 'Best ter look on the bright
side. It could have been worse.'

'Mm, mm,' she mumbled as she heaved her shoulders.
And that's how we had to manage until the landlord
decided to send the men to repair it.

Saturday morning, and Mum was busy getting the car-
rots and herbs ready for the stewpot simmering on the
fire when two workmen came to fix the slates and mend
the door.

'About bloody time!' we heard her call out through the
opening where our door should be.

'Now, now, Polly. No need to carry on. They're here

now,' Dad replied. 'I'd like ter stop and help yer with the door, mate, but I'm in a hurry. Be as quick as yer can. It's freezing in there with the door off.'

'Well,' the feller replied as he stood gazing at it, 'it looks to me as if yer want a new dower, mate, but I'll do wot I can fer the time bein'.'

'Thanks,' Dad replied and hurried away.

As soon as the other chap came down the ladder he called out, 'I've finished on the roof, Joe. Can I 'elp yer with the dower?'

'I don't know 'ow I'm goin' ter get this bloody thing back on its hinges, the bloody wood's rotten!'

When Mum heard him she cried out through the gap, 'Wot yer expect when the thing blew orf its 'inges and was left in a pool of rain all night? Anyway, it's bin rottin' fer years,' she added.

'I wun't be long, missus. Anyway, I'll do me best I can fer the time bein',' he replied.

Mum came back towards the fire, and as she began to stir the pot of stew she told us to lay the table ready for dinner. While we were busy we heard the man call out, 'We're finished, Missus, and that's the best we can do!'

When Mum inspected the door it wouldn't open. As she tugged and pulled it towards her the knob came off in her hand and she yelled through a gap in the doorway, 'Yer better push this bloody door open. It's stuck.' As soon as the workman pulled the door out towards him, Mum nearly went out with it.

'Yer bleedin' fool! Yer've put it on the wrong way!' she yelled.

'That's the best we can do with it. The wood's rotten. Yer lucky we could fix it at all.'

'But what about the gap you've left down the side? Bleedin' codged up job, that's what it is! And I s'pose yo've put the slates on the wrong way an' all. Now I'll 'ave ter wait till it rains ter find out!'

'Well,' replied the other feller, 'if yo ain't satisfied yer better see yer landlord for a new dower!'

'Yes! I'll goo now while yer wait 'ere.'

But as soon as Mum hurried to get her shawl the workmen were gone.

'Katie, Frankie and Liza! Watch that stew don't boil over. I wurn't be long.'

Frankie and I would have liked to have followed Mum to see what was being said, but we knew it was more than we dare do to disobey her.

'You go, Liza,' I said. 'She won't say nothing to you.'

'I'm not going! You both heard what Mum said.'

While the three of us were arguing she came back. We knew the landlord had his business in an old derelict cottage a few yards away in Slone Street, which he called his office.

Mum was fuming. 'Bloody old skinflint! 'E warn't thea! But I'll 'ave 'im when 'e comes for 'is rent next Saturday as sure as God med little apples!' she yelled.

So until the following Saturday we had to plug the gap with old rags to help keep out the cold draughts.

As soon as the landlord came for his rent, Mum was ready for him. He stood on the step and knocked on the door. Mum swung it open suddenly and as he fell flat on his back we saw him stare at us through the open doorway. He got to his feet and dusted himself down with his cap, and Mum began to grin all over her face. 'I'm very sorry, Mr Priest. I fergot to warn yer the dower opens the other way.'

'But I sent two workmen to fix it!' he replied angrily.

'Well, that's 'ow they left it an' they said that's the best they could do cuss the dower's rotten and it would be better if yer fixed me another dower!'

'Did they fix the roof?'

'Well, I see the one called Alf up the ladder, but I can't say until it rains agen. An' let me say this while I'm at it. I ain't payin' no mower rent till I get another dower fixed properly!'

'Very well, Mrs Greenhill. But if I do manage ter find you another door, I not only want my rent paid regular each week, but also some of the arrears. Or you will know what to expect!'

'Very well. Yo get another dower, then I'll think about it.'

'Well, yer better think about it or the next thing you'll be fixed with will be the bailiffs. Now good day!'

As soon as Mum closed the door behind her, she heard Dad coming down the yard. She pushed the door open ready for him. As he came in she cried out, ''E's bin!'

'Who yer on about now?'

'The landlord,' she replied, and began to smile.

When she told him what she had done Dad replied, 'Polly! You want to be careful, he won't take it lightly you knocking him down.'

'I dain't knock him down, the dower done that for me! But he's promised me another.'

'Well, yer better wait and see if it comes.'

'It'ad betta. 'E'll get no rent till it does. Any'ow,' she added, 'yo just mind yer 'ead, Sam, when yer cum in 'an out. I've already banged mine a couple of times, an' even the knob of the dower don't fit properly now.'

Suddenly Frankie piped up, 'Dad, why not chalk a sign on the door outside? "Please don't push. Pull first if yer don't want to get hurt".'

'Let's have none of your funny ideas,' Dad replied. 'Anyway, while you've got yer coat on yer can go ter the paper shop and fetch me the *Punch* and two penn'orth of twist, and ask 'em for a clay pipe, I broke the last one they gave me.'

'An' 'urry back!' Mum called out. 'I don't want yer comin' back an' moanin' agen about the fat settlin' 'ard on yer dinner.'

A week later, a different workman arrived to fix another door. He said it was one from a derelict building, better and stronger than our old one, but first he had to plane it before it fitted. Another feller came the next day to paint it, but when Mum saw the colour she yelled, 'Yer can tek yer 'ook! I ain't 'avin' green, it's me unlucky colour!' That door was never painted but it weathered the storms for as long as I can remember.

Going to School

I shall never forget the 1st of February 1908. I was at the tender age of five and felt happy and grown up to think that I was to start my schooldays.

It was very cold with patches of ice underfoot when my mother helped me to get ready so that she could take me to our local church school at the top of the hill. I was dressed in a shabby, faded brown frock, one of my eldest sister Mary's cut down, which hung almost to my feet. When I complained it was too long, my mother replied, 'Yow'll grow into it.' As I kept staring down at it she shouted in my ear, 'Come on! 'Urry yerself. I ain't got all day to watch yo admire yerself!'

'I wasn't, Mum. It's too long an' I don't like brown an' it's too long,' I repeated.

'Yo'll wear it whatever the colour is! Yer ungrateful, that's wot y'are! Any'ow yo'll grow into it soon enough, 'an yer better stuff some cardboard in yer boats ter keep the wet out, I don't want yer cryin' ter me with yer chilblains!' she added.

After I laced my boots on, she pulled me close to her. 'Now come 'ere an' let's comb yer 'air.'

'I've done it, Mum,' I replied. I knew how often she tugged my hair when she was short tempered. But she only lifted it this time.

'I don't want to see any nits in youse 'air like some kids I know up the yard!'

As soon as she was satisfied, she told me to go and fill the kettle. As I waited for little Billy Kelly to fill his mum's bucket, I heard his mum call out from outside the brewhouse door, 'I've left yer some hot suds in the boiler, Polly.' Before my mum could reply, I saw Billy put his tongue out at her and call out, 'I left yer some suds, Polly.'

Before Mum could reach him, he dropped the bucket and ran. She stamped across the yard, and, facing Billy's mother who was busy drying her wet soapy hands on her hessian apron, she exclaimed, 'Sarah Kelly! If that cheeky lad of yers was a son of mine I'd wallop 'is bloody arse. 'E wouldn't be able to sit down for a wick!'

Mrs Kelly couldn't have heard what her son had said for she looked at Mum as she answered, 'What's 'e bin up ter now, Polly?'

'Yer wanta learn 'im some manners! I'm Mrs Greenhill ter kids, not Polly!'

'I'm sorry but there's no need for yer ter get ratty. Any'ow, I'll speak to 'is father when 'e gets 'ome.'

'Yo see that yer do, Sarah, or else! If I ever see 'im agen I'll smack 'is arse meself.'

'Not while I'm about yer wun't!' she replied angrily. 'Or yer might find me 'avin' yer up in court. I ain't scared of yer, even if all the other neighbours are!'

As Mum snatched the kettle from me and walked towards our house, I heard Mrs Kelly say, 'Bleedin' old rat bag!'

I tremble to think what my mother would have done had she heard her, for she was scared of no one and the neighbours knew it.

As soon as we were indoors I watched her flop down in Granny's old rocking chair. 'Reach me down that tin box off the shelf,' she said.

After sorting out pawn tickets, death policies and other papers, she showed me what she was looking for.

''Ere's yer birth certificate. It's ter prove who yer are an' 'ow old yer are, an' yer ter give it to one of the teachers, an' mind yer manners, always say please or thank yer.'

As I began to read it, she cried out, 'Did yer 'ear wot I said?'

'Yes, Mum,' I replied.

'Right! Now! When yer come out of school after yer lessons I want yer straight back 'ere! An' no dawdlin', yer understand?'

'But what about Liza? She never comes straight home. She always . . .'

'Never yer mind about Liza! There are still yer jobs ter do an' where's that 'anky I give yer?'

'It's in me pinny pocket.'

'Well, use it and wipe yer snotty nose!'

As we started up the hill, she grabbed hold of my

hand. My feet seldom touched those icy cobbles; I remember my mother always did everything at the double, as if she hadn't got time to live. As soon as we arrived at the school door, she looked me over again, then pushing my hair from out of my eyes she cried out impatiently, 'Come on. Yo'll do!'

Just as we were about to enter, we noticed an old man dressed in ragged brown overalls and carrying a bucket of coke, a shovel and an oily piece of rag, step up on to the pavement from a trap door outside the school.

'You'll 'ave ter go in quietly. The lessons 'ave already begun,' I heard him say.

'W'oer you?' my mother asked as she stared down at him.

'I'm the caretaker, Mrs, an' I'm also the 'andy man, me name's Fred an' I feed the boiler ter keep the school pipes hot, I'm also the odd job man, an' if yer want yer chimney swept any time I only charge a shillin',' he replied all in one breath.

''Ave yer finished!' Mum snapped as she shrugged her shoulders and went through the door.

As we entered the long corridor she said, 'Now yo' stay 'ere while I find a teacher.'

The corridor was very narrow, lit by a gas jet surrounded by a wire bracket high on a dark green and brown painted wall, and smelt strongly of Condy's Fluid. Two feet from the ground along one wall was a wooden form beneath which were hot iron pipes, while on the opposite wall there were seven classrooms. I stood on my toes and peered through a frosted glass door, which I could now see was the infants' class. There were about fifty young boys and girls sitting crosslegged on a bare old wooden floor.

Curiosity got the better of me, and as I gently pushed the door a little way open, I noticed an elderly woman sitting at the organ. (This person was to become my music teacher.) I was immediately thrilled when she began to play a lovely little song we kids had learned and sung at the Band of Good Hope and Sunday School, which we attended on Saturdays and Sundays. As soon as the children began to sing I was feeling so happy that I very quietly sang with them, so as not to be heard.

The words to the song went something like this:

> Light a little candle
> Burning in the night
> In this hour of darkness
> So we must shine
> You in your small corner
> And I in mine.

I was ready to sing some more when suddenly I felt a movement behind me, and as I turned around I saw the head teacher and my mum listening. I became very nervous, thinking I would be punished, but the teacher soon put me at my ease when she asked, 'Where did you learn to sing like that, my dear?'

'At the Band of Good Hope and Sunday School,' I replied proudly. As she turned to my mum I heard her say, 'We will have to put Kate in some of our singing classes, Mother.' But Mum didn't answer, she just shrugged her shoulders.

The teacher asked me if I would like to sing later to the infants. 'Oh yes, Miss. I love singing,' I replied excitedly. Suddenly my mother piped up, 'She ain't come 'ere ter sing! She's 'ere ter learn. An' any'ow she does enuff of that at 'ome.'

'I quite understand the concern for your daughter, but her first lesson will be the alphabet, then she will go on from there, as you, may know.'

'I don't know! I never 'ad any schoolin', but I do know she's mower advanced than some of the kids yer learn 'ere.'

'In what way, may I ask?'

'Well, she can read *and* write and spell and she can tell the time!'

'Where did she learn if you say *you* never went to school?'

'Her dad learns 'er an' me other two young'uns.'

'I'm pleased to hear that. It will be an advantage to Kate. Now, if you will please bring her tomorrow morning at nine o'clock. Good morning, Mrs Greenhill. Be happy, Kate, and keep singing,' she added.

I was disappointed that I couldn't stay. 'Can't I stay now, Miss? I'll be awfully . . .' Before I could finish, my mum grabbed hold of my hand and snapped, 'No yer bloody carn't! Yer know I want yer 'elp in the brewhouse!' As I turned around to wish the teacher good morning I saw the frown on her face as she stared hard at my mother again.

When my dad came home that evening, the first thing he asked me was if I'd been to school. 'Yes, Dad. Mum took me,' I replied, 'but I don't really start until tomorrow morning.'

When he asked why, I began to tell him how I sang and what the teacher had said and what Mum said, but I was careful not to say *all* that my Mum had said as I knew he would flare up at her. He then told me that if I behaved and did what the teachers expected of me, I wouldn't go far wrong, but if at any time I was in doubt, he would always be there to help me.

The following morning, dressed in my same old patched brown frock, pinafore and paper-packed boots, I ate my porridge and, as I sat waiting for my mother to take me to school, she said, 'Yo'll 'ave ter goo by yerself. I'm too busy an' I ain't feelin' well, any'ow. They've got all the information they need, an' there'll be plenty of other kids there ter tell yer wot ter do an' who ter see!'

In one way I was pleased she wasn't coming. If she performed like she had the day before, I knew I'd feel awful with all the other children near.

As I started out I saw little Billy Kelly pulling his dog called Bobby along on a piece of string. Billy was often called 'Billy Chatterbox', but he was a lovable little lad; I liked him and loved to hear his patter. Many of the neighbours liked him too. He often made me smile at the funny stories he used to make up.

Billy had a sister who was seven, who always seemed to boss him about. Betty was a pretty girl and she knew it, always showing off. She was so different from her brother in character and looks. Billy was about six years old, with black wavy hair and large brown eyes, with a squint in the left one.

Betty was like her mother, whereas Billy actually

looked like his stepfather. He came up to me and said, 'Hello, Katie, you're going to my school then?'

'Yes, Billy, I am on my way now.'

'But yer too early, we can't go until the bell starts ter ring, and I've got ter give Bobby his morning run.'

Bobby was a small, black, grey and brown rough-haired mongrel, with one blue eye and one speckled brown. All the kids in the street loved him, some of the neighbours too. As I stroked him he began to beg. 'Next time, Bobby, I'll bring you some scraps,' I said.

'He likes you, Katie.'

'I like him too. He's lovely. I wish I could have a dog, but Mum won't let me. She only likes cats.'

Billy laughed. 'Well, Katie, you can always 'ave a lend of Bobby.'

'That's kind, Billy, but it's not the same as having your own. I'll come with you any time when you take Bobby for a walk though.'

'Really? Yer promise? Shall I call for yer Saturday?'

'You'd better not, my mum still remembers when you called her Polly.'

'But that's her name, ain't it?'

'Yes, but you never call married people by their Christian names. It's mister, missus, or sir, or miss, whichever the case maybe. Anyway, I'll forgive you, but promise me you won't cheek my mum again or she'll say it's my fault.'

'I'll remember,' he answered with a cheeky grin. 'My dad don't like Bobby,' he added suddenly.

'Why does he let you keep him then?'

'After Mum had a row with me dad over him, Mum

was determined to keep him. That's when I called him Bobby.'

I was now very curious and wanted to know everything. 'Who gave him to yer?' I asked.

'Nobody dain't give him to me! I think he was lost, but Mum said he looked as if nobody wanted him.'

'Why?'

'Well, one mornin', just as me mum went outside to take the sacking off the cellar head ready for the coalman, we saw little Bobby huddled up, shivering and wet. Me mum carried him inside and gave him a bath and a feed. After that, I asked if I could keep him and she told me yes if me dad agreed.'

'So yer dad didn't mind yer keeping him?'

'Oh yes! He did mind! When he came home and saw Bobby asleep on the mat in front of the fire he yelled and he swore, but I can't repeat swear words any more because Mum said I would never go to heaven.'

'Well, what else did he yell?'

'He yelled, "Where's that (and the swear words) mongrel come from?" When Mum told him, there was a terrible row and Dad said she had ter get rid of the flea-bitten thing. But me mum yelled back at him and told him how she bathed him and found no fleas, and said she was not gain' ter get rid of him! After me mum told me Bobby was mine, I stopped crying.

'After a while, Dad said I could keep him if I dain't let him get under his feet, and ter teach him clean habits and take him far enough from the neighbours' houses and the yard to do his ones and twos, yer know what I mean, Katie?' he grinned.

'Yes, Billy,' I replied, grinning back at him. 'Does yer sister like Bobby?'

'No, I don't think so. Once I saw her kick out at him. When Mum saw her, I heard her say if she caught her again she'd thrash her. Bobby must have remembered though, he wouldn't go near her again.'

Betty and I had played together before, but since she had been sent home from school with nits, my mother forbid me to have anything more to do with her.

'I've gotta go now and take Bobby home before the school bell rings.'

'Shall I come with you?'

'Yes, if yer like.'

We had only gone a few yards when Billy began to panic as the bell rang. 'Oh, Katie! What can I do? I ain't got time ter take him home.'

'I'll take him,' I offered; I had no idea of the rules of the school then.

'Yer can't! We gotta be in the playground before the bell stops,' he whimpered.

As luck would have it, my brother Jack was coming up the hill. I hoped I was doing the right thing when I called out, 'Jack! Jack!' As he hurried over I asked, 'Will yer take Billy's little dog home or he'll be late for school?'

'But why ain't *you* already in school?' Jack asked.

'I've got to see the head teacher first.'

'Yer'd better 'urry yerself then, yer know what yer mum's like. All right, I'll take him.'

As soon as my brother took hold of the string, the dog sat on the wet cobbles looking round for Billy. He wouldn't budge an inch until Jack decided to pick him up in his arms and carry him home.

I caught up with Billy and we arrived in the playground with all the others, just as the bell stopped ringing and the caretaker closed the heavy door. Billy grabbed hold of my hand and led me towards a queue of children. I saw some of the girls staring, wondering who I was.

'Who's 'er, Billy?' I heard one of them ask.

'She's come with me an' I'm showing her what to do.'

Just then there was silence all around as we saw the head mistress. I noticed she was dressed differently from the day before and was carrying a cane. She wore a long, grey dress with leg-o-mutton sleeves and a stiff white high collar. Around her waist was a belt with a bunch of keys hanging from a chain, and pinned to her frock was a gilt bar which told me her name was Miss A. Ford – Head Mistress. She came towards me with a frown and pulled me aside. 'What are *you* doing here? You are *not* to be in the playground!'

'I didn't know where to go, I followed Billy,' I replied.

'Billy who?'

'Billy Kelly, miss.'

'Why didn't your mother bring you?'

'She said she was too busy, miss.'

'She was told to bring you in the front of the school at a quarter to nine, to meet your teacher, and now I find you here, in the infants' playground!'

I was getting very nervous, wondering if she was going to cane me. 'It's not my fault, miss, I'm sorry, miss,' I whimpered.

'Very well,' she replied more gently. 'Just go through that door.' She pointed it out with the cane. 'There you will see another door on your left marked "Study". Go in and wait until I come to you.'

I found the door quite easily, and as it was ajar I knocked. When no one answered I walked in, my feet slipping on the well polished worn lino. The room was almost bare except for several bookshelves. There was a large desk in the middle of the room and on the top I saw an open bible. In the far corner a coal fire was burning in a small fire grate which was surrounded by a brass fireguard. There were also six well worn leather chairs and a tall stool.

I was about to warm my hands when I saw Miss Ford enter the room. I was still nervous.

'Come along, Kate,' she said pleasantly. 'Follow me, and don't look so scared, I'm not such a dragon as the older boys think I am. She smiled down at me.

I walked beside her until she told me to wait in the corridor while she went into the infants' classroom, to speak to their teacher. I was about to warm my feet on the hot water pipes when I saw her coming back with another teacher. I noticed that this teacher was also carrying a bamboo cane, and thinking I was going to be punished for being late, I became scared.

'Kate, I must leave you now with Miss Frost, who will be asking you more questions before she takes you into the classroom,' said Miss Ford. What a relief when I saw the cane being handed over to Miss Ford.

While they were both whispering together, I noticed that Miss Frost was a small, dumpy, elderly person, with sharp features and steel-rimmed glasses that she kept pushing up her long, thin nose. She looked very severe with her grey hair pushed back from her high forehead. She was wearing a long brown skirt and white frilly blouse with a high-boned stiff lace collar and leg-o-mutton sleeves. As soon as I was left alone with her I thought to myself, I ain't going to like this one.

'Follow me!' she said abruptly. As we entered a small bare room I noticed it only had one ladderback chair and a desk. She drew a piece of paper from the drawer of the desk and said, 'You may sit down,' then handed me the paper and a pencil. 'Why didn't your mother bring you?' she asked.

'I already explained to the head mistress, miss,' I replied nervously. Suddenly I saw her frown at me over the top of her glasses. 'Well, I am asking you!' she snapped. After my explanation she said, 'I have been told you can already read and write and do sums. Is that true? If so I . . .'

'Yes, miss, but I . . .'

'Don't interrupt!' she snapped, as she pushed her glasses further up her nose. I was becoming more and more nervous and felt very weepy.

'I will leave you to write down what you wish and I'll come back in a few minutes.'

I didn't know what she wanted me to write, so I thought it best to write my name and address. I wrote (hoping this would please her), 'My name is Kate Greenhill, I live with my mother and father, and my sisters and brothers at 26 Camden Grove. My age is five years old and we are very poor because my dad can't get work.' I was about to write more when I saw her enter with the head mistress.

'Well, Kate,' the head said, 'let me see what you have written.'

As they read it, I looked up to see them both smiling. 'You are very good and I am also pleased to see that you join each letter together,' Miss Frost remarked. When they left, I felt better knowing that they were pleased with me.

Soon they were back again to tell me I was to go home. 'But miss, I thought I was to join the infants' class?'

'You won't be joining Standard One. Miss Frost and I have decided you will take your first lessons in Standard Two. You can go home now and tell your dad that we are very pleased with you and that you are to be in line with the six-year-olds at nine o'clock tomorrow morning. Now run along.'

As soon as I arrived home I noticed no one was in. I put the kettle on and was about to make a pot of tea when Mum came through the door.

'Why ain't yer at school?' she bawled.

When I tried to explain she looked as though she didn't believe me. 'I 'ope yer tellin' me the truth or yer know what to expect!'

'If you don't believe me, Mum, you can come with me in the morning.'

'Very well, now tek that kettle off the fire before it burns bloody dry! An' 'urry with that cuppa tea afor yer dad comes in.'

But Dad was already standing in the doorway. When he saw me he started on at Mum. 'What's she doing? I thought I told you to see that she went to school.'

'She went,' Mum replied. 'Now she's tried to tell me some cock an' bull story that they sent 'er 'ome 'til termorra morning.'

'That's the truth, Dad.'

'Very well, love, let's have that cup of tea and no more arguing from you, Polly. If the teacher sent her home till termorrow, I believe her.'

'Oh, well,' she replied, shrugging her shoulders. 'I'd betta get ter the brew'ouse an' finish me washin'. Yer can bring me cup a tea, Katie.'

After Mum had left, Dad asked me what had happened about the teachers. When I told him he said, 'I'm very proud of you and I believe you, even if your mum don't.'

'But me mum doesn't ever believe me.'

'She does really but she's a funny way of showing it. She don't seem to believe *me* sometimes, but I don't blame her too much. She's had so many lies told to her in the past, and a very hard life when she was young.'

'Is it because she can't read or write?' I asked.

'It's a lot to do with that, love, and how she was brought up. Anyway, I'll explain to you when you're older, then maybe you'll understand. Now let's have that cup of tea and take your mum one. You know how she'll grumble if it's cold.'

When I came back with the empty cup he said, 'I don't want you to tell your mother what we've been talking about, otherwise you know what a temper she's got.'

'Yes, Dad, I promise I won't tell her.'

'Now reach me down me clay pipe and fetch two-penn'orth of twist and here's a halfpenny for yerself.'

I put the coin down my black woollen stocking where Mum wouldn't find it. I always saved these farthings and halfpennies, and when I had enough I often bought marbles for Frankie and me. We had to hide these from Mum too.

Next morning I was up early, and after Mum had found me more odd jobs to do I sat down to eat my porridge. When she asked me what Dad had said to me the night before I had my answer ready. 'He asked me about the teachers and I told him I was going in class two and he said I was clever, Mum, and . . .'

'Yo ain't any cleverer than any of the others so don't yer be showin' any airs an' graces! Now yer betta 'urry yerself before the bell starts ringing.'

I was glad to get up from the table and go outside into the yard where I saw little Billy Kelly on his way to school, alone.

'Where's Bobby?' I asked.

'Bobby ain't well,' he whimpered.

'What's the matter with him?'

'When I took him for his walk he kept hangin' behind and draggin' his bum on the cobbles. When I picked him up and took him back home me mum said she was goin' to the chemist ter buy 'im a worm cake. Do yer think he's goin' ter die, Katie?'

'No, yer silly Billy, all dogs have worms.'

'How do you know? *You* ain't got a dog!'

'My eldest sister who lives in Graham Street, she's got

two and they had worms. Now come on and wipe your eyes or we'll be late.'

As we walked up the hill hand in hand, he asked me why he didn't see me yesterday in the playground.

'I don't really start me lessons until today,' I told him.

'Will yer be in my class, Katie?' he asked eagerly.

'I don't know. I got to see the head mistress first. She said I might start in Standard Two.'

'Standard Two? Yer must be very clever then, 'cause yer don't go there till yer six an' I'm older than you!'

When I asked how old he was he said he was six and a half. 'But why haven't you moved up from the infants' class?' I asked.

'Well,' he replied, 'this is the first school I've been to.'

I knew the Kelly family had come to live in our yard about five weeks ago, which was just after Christmas time.

'Didn't you go to school where you used to live?'

'No, me mum and me stepfather was always moving,' he answered.

'But what about the school board man?'

'I don't know about 'im. Any'ow, we'll be movin' agen soon, but it's a secret, so don't tell anybody, Katie, 'cause me mum don't want the neighbours ter know yet.'

'You're not making this up are you?' I asked.

'No, Katie, on me honour. Last night they thought I was asleep, when I 'eard me dad say, "We'll 'ave ter start packin' soon Aggie, afore the bailiffs come." When we leave 'ere will yer mum let me come an' see yer, an' Bobby?' he added.

'Yes, I think so, but you must promise me yer won't cheek my mum agen or she'll never forgive you or me for being friends, but she's not always in a bad temper, only when anything goes wrong. Now I have ter go, I'll see you in the playground later.'

As I let go his hand, I hurried towards the corridor feeling sad; I was only just getting used to my little friend and Bobby. Coming near the classroom I saw another teacher watching me. She approached me and said, 'I believe you are my new girl, Kate Greenhill, correct?'

'Yes, miss,' I replied nervously.

'I'm your teacher: Miss Lester. Who was the boy you were holding hands with? Your brother?'

'No, miss. His name's Billy Kelly who lives in our yard. He's in Standard One, miss.'

'Oh yes, I remember. Now follow me to your classroom, but before we go in I must warn you there are lots of rules. No talking or whispering during lessons, or looking over the next girl's notes and copying. But I don't think I need to tell you, Kate. I have already heard what you can do from the head mistress.'

It was then that I started to lose some of my nervousness.

This was the first time I had been inside a classroom. There were no individual desks as there are today, nor did we wear any type of school uniform. The clothes we wore were whatever our parents had managed to cut down from old clothes until I, and other children like me, were old enough to apply for the *Daily Mail* issue of boots and clothes supplied by the Police Fund. I still remember that old brown patched frock.

As I entered the classroom I noticed several well worn dark forms. Each one had a lean-to with a long slat for pens, four ink wells and crock ink pots. Seated on each form were four girls in a row, many of whom I knew slightly. Each one stared at me as I was told to sit next to the third girl on my right.

Once I was seated my teacher said very sternly to the class, 'This is our new girl. Her name's Kate Greenhill. Now I want you all to make her your friend. Any trouble or bickering, you will answer to me! Now to begin our lessons.' She started to chalk on the blackboard.

During the next few days I began to settle down; I got along well with some of the girls but many I did not. I suppose it was because my hand often shot up first to answer questions that my teacher asked. I also received top marks for some words I happened to spell correctly (thanks to my dad).

A week later I noticed the Kellys' house was empty; they had done a moonlight flit, which was very common in those days. Sad to say I never saw little Billy or his dog Bobby again, but each time I went to Sunday School I often said a little prayer for them.

Rabbit Stew

One very cold afternoon, it was raining heavily as I made my way home from school. As soon as I got indoors Mum called out, 'Don't tek yer coat orf. I want yer to goo fer an errand.'

'But Mum! Can it wait until it's stopped raining? Me hair's all wet and me boots are letting water in.'

'No, it can't wait! I want a loaf afore yer dad gets in. Any'ow, rain water's good fer yer. Now 'urry yerself.'

Just as I was ready to leave there came a loud knock on the door. Mum lifted the corner of the curtains to see who it was, and cried, 'It's yer gran agen!' But before I could open the door, my gran had let herself in.

I remember Gran always wore her well-worn Salvation Army uniform, which she must have had for many years, even before I was born. She seldom went to the Mission, only when it suited her or to hear the gossip. She was a contrary woman, but I loved her. She was the only person I knew who stood up to my mother. 'Right's right an' blood's thicker than water' was one of her sayings when she was angry.

She made her way towards the fireplace and squatted down on the old rocking chair. When she saw the pot of stew simmering on the fire she began to sniff. 'Summat smells good, Polly,' she said, sniffing again.

'Yo alwis know! An' wot yer doin' out on a day like this?' Mum snapped.

'I was just passin', Polly, so I thought I'd call an' see 'ow yer are.'

'It seems to me, Hannah, yer always passin' when yer smell summat cookin'.'

'What did yer say, Polly?'

'Yo 'eard! Yo ain't sa deaf as yer mek out!' Mum snapped.

'Summat smells nice, Polly,' Granny aid again, as she sat back in the rocking chair.

'Well, I ain't got none ter spare terday!' Mum shouted.

'There's no need ter shout, I ain't deaf.'

'Any'ow,' Mum said, 'Sam won't be 'ome for another 'alf 'our.'

'I can wait.'

'Yo 'eard that, yer crafty old bugger!' Mum exclaimed.

Whether Granny heard or not, she dragged the rocker closer to the fire, and as she placed her feet on the steel fender she mumbled, 'I'll 'ave ter goo see the Army Captain, ter find me another pair of old boots. These are letting in the wet.'

I was feeling sorry for her, sitting there in the rocking chair looking so forlorn.

I could see she couldn't get warm enough, so I tried to push the rocker even closer towards the fire. Mum yelled, 'She's near enuff! Unless yer want ter set 'er alight. Any'ow, wot yer doin' gorpen with yer mouth wide open?'

'I was waiting for you to tell me what to fetch.'

'Here's fourpence ter fetch two fly papers an' a loaf, an' yer can see yer gran part of the way 'ome.'

'I ain't ready ter goo yet! Me legs still feel cold,' Granny replied.

As Granny pulled her frock up higher, I heard Mum say, 'It looks ter me as if yo'll need plenty of Fullers Earth rubbed on 'em. Yer got red tram lines on yer legs!'

'I'll goo wen I'm ready!' Granny snapped back.

'Oh well, yer betta stay now. I can see Sam cummin' up the yard.' Mum gave in.

As I hurried out to the grocer's I almost bumped into my dad who asked where I was rushing off to. When I told him he said for me to hurry before it began to rain again.

The loaf was twopence-halfpenny for two pounds in weight. Often it was put on the scales and if it didn't come to standard another piece of bread was put with it; this was called a 'make-weight'. Fly papers for our kitchen were two a penny.

I hurried back and gave Mum the change. I saw the usual counting on her fingers as I heard my dad and gran arguing. 'You ought to have more sense than to listen to gossip, Mother.'

'It's true,' Gran replied. 'Tilly Ruskin told me when I was 'angin' out me washin'.' Now I was all ears.

'Did you know about it, Sam?' Mum piped up.

'Yes, I did hear, but they're not going to wait for the bailiffs, they're doin' a moonlight flit.'

It was then that I knew they were talking about the Turner family, who had only been living in the Kellys' empty house for two months before the neighbours started to gossip.

'Oh God 'elp 'em, I 'ope we never come ter that agen, Sam,' Mum said.

'Now, Polly, and you, Mother, no more gossip so keep yer mouths buttoned. It may only be a rumour.'

Mum and Granny said no more, but Granny kept sniffing and looking at the pot simmering on the hob.

As Dad sat down to read the *War Cry*, Mum began to dish out the stew, and I noticed she was only dishing out a small portion for Granny. As soon as she noticed it I expected Gran to grumble, but she just gave Mum enough black looks to kill her.

'Yer can fill yerself with plenty of bread, Hannah,' Mum said. She took two thick pieces and broke it up into the gravy.

As soon as we'd finished our meal, Granny was ready to go, but Dad got up from the table and fetched a basin from the cupboard. Mum looked at him daggers as he began to fill the dish with broth and vegetables. 'What's that for?' she asked.

'It's for Mother,' Dad replied.

'Ain't she 'ad enough?'

'She's to take it home with her. Now, come on, Mother, before it starts to rain agen. I'll see *you* later, Polly!' I knew there was going to be more rows when he returned.

Dad came back an hour later looking the worse for drink. As soon as he came in he began to shout. 'I suppose yer thought I dain't see what yer served my mother?'

'Well, I give 'er wot we could spare. Any'ow, she 'elped 'erself ter plenty of bread. An' another thing, there wouldn't 'ave bin enough for the others.'

'Why didn't yer give her some off your plate? I saw you serve enough for yourself. Even the cats are given more than yer give my mother!'

'The cats always 'ave a penn'orth of lights. Anyway she always meks believe she's passin' the dower when 'er smells the pot!'

'Well, you'll treat her differently next time she calls or yo'll answer ter me! Where's Liza and Frankie?'

'They're next door at a party,' I piped up.

'Well, yer better call 'em, Katie, an share the washing up.'

When I knocked on Mrs Buckle's door, I called out, 'Frankie and you Liza! Yer better come now.'

'We ain't coming yet!' I heard Liza reply.

'You'd *better* come, unless yer want me dad to fetch yer!'

'All right, we're coming,' they both replied.

As soon as we'd been given our orders to wash and wipe the dishes we heard Dad bounce out of the house. When he had gone Mum said for us to leave what we were doing and go up to bed.

I knew many of the rows at home were caused by Mum's meanness and temper when she didn't have enough money to eke out for food. Although we all knew Dad would walk miles to find any kind of work, sometimes he would stay out for days, but he never gave up trying to get odd jobs to do. Some days when he was lucky enough to earn a few shillings, he was able to give Mum extra. When this happened we would have rabbit stew, which was often topped up for the rest of the week with bacon bones, pigs' trotters, pork scratchings or mutton bones. The pot was often simmering on the hob from Monday till Saturday, always with some concoction added. If we didn't eat it, it was put in front of us again until we were too hungry to refuse. Some Saturdays we might be lucky enough to have tripe and onions, or liver and bacon, or chitterlings. Other mornings Mum would go early to the meat market, sometimes to buy six penn'orth of pieces for Sunday dinner. If she was lucky she would bring home a thick piece of hipbone steak which the butcher couldn't sell because it had fallen off the block and got covered with wet sawdust.

Sometimes it would be a pig's head, and after Mum had singed the hairs off with a lighted piece of paper, she would scrape the brains out to be spread on toast. The rest would be boiled and the gravy from that would go into our weekly simmering pot. Nothing was ever wasted or discarded. Mum always found some use for everything. As soon as the pig's head was ready she would strip all the meat off and put it into a large basin, which she would turn upside down with the heavy iron on top. Next day this set to brawn, ready for other meals or sandwiches. The bones were never thrown away either. They too went into the pot. Often I would hear my mum say, 'Waste not want not an' wot we ain't got we'll 'ave ter goo without.'

Some of our happier times were the journeys home from Sunday School or the Band of Hope. We would hear and see the muffin man calling out, 'Muffins, muffins, three a penny muffins, all fresh muffins.' Then there was the periwinkle man. 'Periwinks! Tuppence a pint! All fresh boiled terday. Periwinks, periwinks, come and get yer periwinks.' My dad would sometimes go without his baccy to give us a treat of those periwinks. Sitting on the mat in front of the fire, how our mouths would water as Mum sat facing us with the basin of vinegar on her lap. She would watch every winkle we picked out with a pin, and even boiled the empty shells to get the last drop of juice.

On Saturday mornings we would see our jolly old coalman delivering his coal. He was always dressed in the same old black shabby coat which almost touched the floor. He also wore a battered felt hat. His round, jolly face had a bulbous nose and mutton-chop side whiskers, and you would always hear him singing a little ditty as he drove his horse and wagon.

I still remember the words to that ditty:

> Slap, slap, goes me whip,
> I whistle and I sing,
> While upon me wagon,
> I'm as happy as a king,
> O, me horse is always willing,
> Me, I'm never sad,
> None could be as happier,
> As Jim the Carter's lad.

After delivering the coal he would lead the horse to the water trough, then give us kids a ride on his wagon back to the wharf.

Then there was the rag-and-bone man; this name suited him too. He looked as though he hadn't seen soap or water since the midwife washed him. No one knew his name, so he was often called Moocher, always sorting through miskins or dustbins. He lived alone in Slone Street, a few yards from our Camden Grove, in an old hut, part of a derelict coal yard. Often he'd be seen with an old bassinet overloaded with rags, bones, old iron, rusty kettles and old battered buckets. Sometimes you would see him with a loaned-out old flat hand cart overloaded with iron bedsteads, flock beds and even straw mattresses for the farmer's manure.

In the Family Way

On Saturday nights crowds of people of all ages could be seen hustling and bustling towards the open-air meat market in the Bull Ring to get the very best bargains of cheap meat and vegetables from the barrow boys. I often used to go with my little sister Liza and Frankie to pick up all the fruit and sometimes vegetables that would otherwise be swept away.

I was about six years of age when my mother took me with her one Saturday night to help carry whatever she could buy or beg. As we walked up the stone steps I saw crowds of people gathered together waiting to be served. The noise was deafening as everybody tried to push their way towards the meat stall.

The butcher was a jolly feller, almost giving away the leftovers, but people began to grumble as my mother jostled among the crowd, dragging me with her. We found ourselves up at the front when I heard: 'Yow, get at the back, we was 'ere fust!' Then the others joined in, shouting and swearing. Ignoring their insults, Mum yelled, 'I was 'ere befower any of yow lot! But I warn't gooin' ter miss me turn 'cus I 'ad ter goo ter the closet!' (How she lied!)

As the butcher served her with a breast of mutton and some scrag ends of meat, there were still arguments. The butcher handed over the meat and I heard him say, ''Ere y'ar', Mrs Greenhill, an' tek yer bloody turn next time or I won't serve yer agen!' As she stood there counting the change on her fingers from her half-crown, a large buxom woman made her way towards her. I was scared, for I knew what some of these women were capable of. As she came up to my mum I knew there was going to be trouble.

'Oh, if only my dad was here,' I kept thinking when I saw her push Mum and yelled for all to hear, 'Yer old cow! It ain't the first time yo've jumped the queue!' Suddenly she lashed out and punched and pushed her fist in Mum's face. 'An' let that be a lesson to yer!'

I began to scream, and hung on to her skirt but she flung me away.

As my mother hurried off she yelled, 'I'll get yo, Lizzie Mitchell, when I see yer agen in the pawn shop, if it's the larst thing I do. You old bag.'

Crowds began to gather to see what all the commotion was; I was still whimpering as Mum made her way to the fish stalls. I noticed her eye was beginning to look red and swollen. Luckily there were no other customers when she asked the young fishmonger for some herrings. I saw him smile. 'Who's gid yer that?' he asked as he pointed to Mum's left eye.

'Never yo mind! I want a pound of 'errin's with soft roe!'

'You'll 'ave ter take pot luck, missus, I can't see inside 'em.'

'None of yower bloody cheek neither! An' 'ave yer got a cod fish's 'ead yer can give me?' She smiled more calmly.

'You'll need more than soft roe or a cod's head ter put on that shiner! Anyway, here's a couple, and a few sprats ter go with 'em.'

Mum walked away with her fish and meat parcels, and as she dropped them into the carrier bag she called out, 'Cheeky young bleeda!' I hated going anywhere with my mother, she was so cantankerous and argumentative. On the way home she warned me not to tell my dad or anyone how she had won her black eye. If he should ask I was to say that she fell down the market steps. I hoped I didn't have to lie; luckily for me I didn't.

As soon as we arrived indoors we saw Dad sitting by the fire reading the *War Cry*. He looked up and saw Mum's eye. 'How yer come by that?' he asked.

'I fell down the market steps, an' if yo'd 'ave bin with me this wouldn't 'ave 'appened!'

'I've told yer before, Polly, when yer stop counting on yer fingers and trust people I'll come shopping with you anytime, so let's have no more arguing. I've got some good news ter tell yer. Now the kettle's on the boil so Katie can make a pot of tea while *you* sit down and listen to what I have to say.'

As they sat down facing each other, I listened eagerly.

'Well, let's 'ear it!' Mum said impatiently.

'I have found me a permanent job at last, Polly.'

'Thank God fer that!' she cried, changing her tune.

'Now listen ter what I've got ter tell yer and don't interrupt!' Mum was all ears. 'It's brick laying.'

'But I didn't know yer could do brick layin'.'

'I was a brick maker when I was only fourteen. That's when I lived in London. After there was no work to be found, I came back to Birmingham. Now this job means leaving here ter work in Manchester.'

Suddenly Mum flung her arms around him and kissed him. But as she released him she cried out, 'Manchester? Why Manchester? 'Ow yer goin' ter get there?'

'There's a feller I was talking to and he's bringing the lorry Monday to pick us up.'

'We? Who's we? We ain't about ter leave 'ere agen are we, Sam?'

'No, yer silly woman. Me an' Bill Owens an' George Tyler. Now listen while I finish. I'm told the wages are good but it means we might be moving from one town to another, which means I won't be able to come home every night or weekends or even for weeks, but yer won't be short. I'll send yer some money each week and I'll write and let you know how I'm faring.'

'But I carn't read or write! Yer know that, Sam.'

'That's a job for Katie to do.'

'But I won't know where to write to you, Dad,' I piped up.

'I'll send you the address and where I'm staying. Now, Polly,' he added, 'yer better make a paste of Fullers Earth and dab it on that eye before it turns black.'

She threw her arms round Dad's neck again and

kissed him, and as she did so he winked at her and said, 'I'll want more than that, Polly, later on.'

I don't think I ever saw Mum more contented than that Saturday night. After they had been whispering together, they made their way towards the stairs and on the way up I saw Dad pinch her bottom. Mum saw me staring and cried out, 'Won't be long, Katie! Keep the tea 'ot. We're goin' to sort yer dad's clothes out.'

I thought they were a long time packing, for Dad didn't have much in the way of clothes, just a pair of woollen combinations, a woollen vest and a couple of well-patched union shirts, a grey coat and a waistcoat, not forgetting the old Army coat he brought back from the Boer War. As I opened the stairs door to call out that their tea was getting cold, I heard my mother giggling. I was too young and too innocent then to realise what they were really doing.

On the Monday morning I was awake early. As soon as I heard the lorry drive up outside our entry I dressed quickly, and when I got downstairs I saw tears in my mum's eyes. 'Where's me Dad?' I yelled, thinking he had gone without saying goodbye. I began to cry.

''E ain't gone yet. 'E's in the shed sortin' out 'is tools,' said Mum.

When he came out I threw my arms around him and wept.

'Now, now, don't upset yerself, love, I'm not going away for ever, I'll be back before you'll even forget me.'

'I'll never forget you, Daddy, but I wish you wasn't going far away an leaving us.'

'Me too,' Mum said.

As he walked towards the old mud-splashed lorry, he suddenly turned back and took me in his arms again and, as he hugged and kissed me, I heard the driver say, 'Would yer like yer daughter to ride on top with yer to the end of the street?'

Dad lifted me over the side and I sat on his lap between Mr Owens and another elderly man. I turned and looked back at Mum and I saw her with her apron to her eyes. As the driver turned the corner into Cavendish Street, Dad lifted me down on to the pavement and as the lorry drove away I sat on the edge of the pavement and wept.

As the weeks went by, money and letters from my dad were few and far between, and when Mum fell ill I wasn't able to go to school. When I cried and kept asking to go she went wild. 'Yer ken wait! Yer more useful ter me around the 'ouse.'

'But what about the school board man?'

'I'll deal with 'im!'

'But me dad said I should go.'

'Well, yer dad ain't 'ere ter find out. An' I 'ope yer don't tell 'im neither!'

Some days she was very quiet, and then I noticed she was beginning to look pale. I asked if I could fetch or do anything for her.

'Yer can mek me a cuppa hot tea and yer can fetch me a Sedlitz powder and some castor oil from the chemist. If 'e asks, tell 'im it's fer yer Mum's bad stumach.' Although I really didn't love my mother, I didn't like to see her ill. I ran all the way to Snapes the chemist in Great Hampton Street, where I ran into my gran.

'Where are you off to?' she asked.

'To the chemist for Mum,' I said.

'Why ain't yer at school?'

'Mum said I had to stay away because she's ill.'

'Well, get what yer come for an' I'll come back with yer,' said Gran.

As soon as we got back to the house, Mum began to shout, 'Wot yo want! It ain't pot yer can smell terday, 'cuss I ain't well enuff ter cook!'

'Katie says yer poorly, an' by the look of yer, yer should be in bed,' said Gran.

'I'll be all right termorra.'

'What's been the matter with yer then?'

'I've been sick two mornings, Hannah. I'm afraid, er, er . . .'

'No! I can't believe it, Polly. At yer age an' all.'

'Wot's me age gotta do with it? I'm only forty-seven.'

'It's a lot ter do with it! An 'e should 'ave bin careful.'

I wondered what they were having high words about. 'Is it me dad you're talking about?' I asked.

'No,' Granny replied. 'And yo listen ter me. Go an' play outside. This is women's talk, I'll call yer in wen I'm ready to leave!'

'I don't wanta go outside and play, I wanta know about me dad.'

'Yo listen ter me! It's not for your ears so do as yer told!'

Half-heartedly I moved towards the door, when Mum began to yell, 'Move yerself befower *I* clout yer one!'

Just as I got to the door she pushed me outside and closed it behind me, but I could hear every word through the crack as they raised their voices.

'Now, Polly, are yer really sure?'

'I've 'ad enough kids ter know. An' don't yell at me!'

'Well, yer should be ashamed of yerself. I can't see why yer let 'im? Yo've refused 'im often enuff.'

'It warn't my fault, I didn't think 'e'd leave it in. If I dain't let 'im in 'e'd tek it somewhere else, an' I wouldn't be surprised if 'e's got some floosie ter tec 'is fancy!'

'Not my Sam, 'e was brought up properly!' Granny yelled.

''E's a man ain't 'e! Any'ow, will yer get me some Slippery Elm, an' Penny Royal, an' Pikery Pills, an' don't ferget the gin,' Mum said.

'Who's gooin' ter pay for it?'

'Don't worry, I'll give it yer out of the rent.'

'All right, but whatever 'appens don't tell anybody, nor Sam. 'E'd never fergive me. I'll see yer next wick.'

I still had my ear to the crack when the door was suddenly flung open and I fell inside the room. As I lay sprawled on the floor, my granny took my drawers down and slapped my bottom hard.

'Now yo've 'eard all that, you'd betta keep it under yer tongue, or else. An' if yer don't, an' yer dad finds out, there'll be trouble for me an' yer mum!'

'I promise I won't say a word to anybody, Granny,' I whimpered.

As she picked me up from the floor, I heard Mum say, 'Yer can be sure she won't breathe a word, Hannah. She'll know what to expect from me otherwise! Now get yer coat on, I want yer to fetch an errand, and stop yer blartin'!' she said to me. At that moment Granny left saying she had to hurry before the landlord called. After she had gone, Mum said I had to go to the grocer's for two penn'orth of bacon bones to top the pot up.

'An' tell 'im not ter shave the bacon off this time!'

When she put the silver threepenny piece inside a piece of paper she said, 'See's as yer don't lose it or yer know what yer get. An' don't ferget to ask 'im fer a penny change.'

Scared in case I did lose it, I squeezed the paper tightly in my hand. In case I forgot what I had been sent for, I kept saying, 'Two penn'orth of bacon bones and a penny change.' People passing kept staring at me as I repeated my errand out loud. As soon as I entered the shop I saw one of Mum's neighbours.

''Ello, Katie, why ain't yer at school?' she asked.

'Me mum's not well an' I've got to hurry, Mrs Taylor.'

'Well, yer betta serve her, I can wait,' she said to Mr Baker.

'What is it you've come for this time?'

'Mum wants two penn'orth of bacon bones and she says yer not to shave 'em.'

'Let's see the colour of yer money then, and none of yer cheek!'

When I gave him the piece of paper, he took out the silver threepenny piece and as he handed over the parcel of bones I stood there waiting for the penny change, when he asked, 'What yer waitin' for?'

'Me penny change, please.'

'You tell yer mum she still owes me tuppence for the last lot, so that'll be a penny off the slate!'

'I can't, Mr Baker, she won't believe me.'

'Well, you tell her ter come herself!'

Disappointed and worried what my mum was going to say, I walked out with the parcel. I had only gone a few yards when Mrs Taylor followed me. 'Here's a penny and don't say anything ter yer mum, nor about what the grocer said, yer know what yer mum's like.' After I thanked her I told her I would give the penny back from my savings.

'That's all right. You keep it.'

'But what if me mum finds out?'

'If she does you just leave it to me.'

Two days later she knocked on our door. As soon as she entered I heard her say, 'I hope you don't mind me telling yer, Polly, but if yer want a betta two penn'orth of bacon bones, yer want ter get 'em from Stoddards, the pork butcher, and you'll get more than that skinflint gives yer.'

'That's all right fer yer to say, but they don't let out strap!'

'I know, but yer a customer, ain't yer?'

'Yes,' Mum replied. 'I buy me tripe an' cow-'eels.'

'Well then, yer know the Stoddards I mean, the one on the corner of Carver Street and Icknield Street where the pigs are slaughtered?'

'Thanks for tellin' me, Agnes, I know where it is.'

As soon as she had gone, Mum gave me twopence. 'Now 'urry before they're sold out.' I was pleased and so was she when I came back with twice as many bones and bacon bones with mould.

Early the following Monday morning I was surprised to see my granny on the doorstep. 'Ain't yer mum up yet?' she asked as she came into the room.

'No, Granny. She don't get up till I've took her tea and toast up.'

As she walked towards the stairs, Grannie cried out, 'Well, she can come down an' get 'er own toast an' tea for a change.'

'But, Granny, she'll . . .'

'Never you mind what she'll say! Yo just leave it and get yerself washed an' ready, I'm tekin' yer to school.'

As I put the kettle on the fire I heard her shout from the bottom of the stairs again. 'Yer betta come down, Polly. There's summat I wanta say.'

When Mum came downstairs my granny attacked. 'Yer should be ashamed of yerself, lyin' in bed ter be waited on when Katie should be at school. Any'ow I'm mekin' sure she goes this time. I'm tekin' 'er meself!'

'Which school are yer thinkin' of tekin' 'er to then?' Mum replied calmly.

'To Camden Drive, where she's registered!' snapped Granny.

'I thought she could go to the same school as Liza and Frankie in Nelson Street.'

'It's too late, she's gooin' ter the school where she'll meet other young girls and people she knows.'

So it was decided I would go back to Camden Drive School. How happy I felt that spring morning, when I saw how pleased my teacher was to see me.

Dad Goes Missing

Weeks went by and Mum was getting bigger and more irritable. She and my granny had already notified the police about my dad and where he'd been staying in digs in Manchester, but we never heard from them. Gran said no news was good news, but if she didn't hear from him or the police in another few days time, she was going to Manchester herself. Mum had already pawned everything she could lay her hands on, and when there was nothing left she applied to Unit Street Parish Relief Rooms for help. The inquisitors came and looked through the rooms, even the bedroom and attic, until they were satisfied we needed help.

When I came back with our allotted groceries, I saw and heard our neighbour, Mrs Owens, indoors talking to Mum.

'Yo sure yo 'aint 'eard, Polly?' I heard her say.

'No,' replied Mum. 'But 'is mother is thinkin' of travellin' ter Manchester ter find out.'

'Manchester! Why that's miles away. Where's 'er gooin' ter get the money from ter goo ter Manchester?' Mrs Owens asked.

'Yer betta ask 'er yerself. She's 'ere now.'

As Gran walked through the door Mrs Owens demanded, 'An' wot do *yo* want? Come ter gloat over Polly's misfortune? I've come ter see if Polly 'ad heard from Sam 'cuss *I* ain't 'eard from Bill.'

'Well, ye've got yer answer. So if I do decide ter goo an' find my son, it won't be for your benefit! Now clear orf. We don't want your sort around 'ere!' Granny said.

'I ain't goin', yer miserable old bible puncher!'

Before Granny could get to her, Mrs Owens was out of the door as quick as lightning.

Mrs Owens must have waited until Granny had gone, for later on I saw her coming back across the yard making straight for our house. As she knocked on the door I cried out, 'It's Mrs Owens agen, Mum.' I could see Mum was in one of her nasty moods.

'I wunda what she wants agen! Nosy old bag! Any'ow, yer gotta let 'er in befower the neighbours' curtains start swishin'.'

As soon as she walked in, Mrs Owens said, 'I dain't mean ter upset yer mother-in-law, Polly, but I know she don't like me.'

'Can yer wunda why when yer livin' in sin!'

'I know yer think that but it's not wot yer think, they're me two cousins.'

'Don't kid me, Lizzie Owens! I warn't born yersterday!

I know and so do the neighbours that they're yer fancy-men yer sleep with!'

'Oh well, they're only jealous!' she replied, shrugging her shoulders.

'Well, God 'elp yer if Bill ever finds out. If 'e does come back, there'll be blood an' snot flyin' about,' Mum said.

'I 'ave who I like in my 'ouse an' I won't be seen in the Parish Rooms or at the three brass balls with me belly up. Anyway, why can't yer sons 'elp, an' yer daughter, Mary?'

Suddenly Mum stood up and faced her, her face all red with anger. 'Yo leave my family out of this and mind yer own bloody business, yo old bag! Now clear orf before I throw summat at yer!'

I knew my mum was quite capable of doing anything when she was in an angry mood, and I was beginning to get scared they might come to blows. I knew my mother often beat me, maybe I deserved it at times, and I hated her for it, but I wasn't going to stand by and see her hurt in her condition. She was my mum after all was said and done. But when she saw me pick up the poker, she yelled, 'What yer think yer gooin' ter do with that? Put it down at once!'

Mrs Owens saw it was best to leave, so heaved her huge shoulders and bounced out of the house. As soon as the door banged shut behind her, my mum pulled me towards her and yelled in my ear, 'If I ever see yer pick up that poker to anyone agen I'll skin yer alive.'

'But Mum, I thought . . .'

'Never yer mind what yer thought! Just remember what I said. Now get yer coat on an' tell yer granny I need 'er *now*. I don't feel well.'

I ran all the way. As Granny opened the door a little way, I could see she was still wearing her old faded Salvation Army uniform, although she only attended when it suited her.

'Well, what do yer want now?' she called out irritably as she opened the door wider. 'Yer better come in out of the cold, and why ain't yer at school?'

'It's our Easter holiday, Granny, and Mum wants yer to come now, Granny,' I cried out all in one breath.

'Don't keep callin' me "Granny", I'm sick of 'earin' the name. In future I'd like yer to call me "Gran" or "Grandma".'

'Yes, Grandma,' I replied.

'Now! What's the matter with yer mum this time?'

'Mrs Owens's been upsetting me mum again and they nearly came to blows, Granny.'

'Where is she now?'

'She left in a huff, Granny.'

'Wait 'ere while I feed me cats. Yer lucky ter find me in, I was just off ter the Mission.' I helped feed her cats, then she tied on her bonnet and shut the door.

As soon as we arrived home, Granny cried out, 'What's the trouble now, Polly?'

'That trollop's bin 'ere agen, askin' if I'd 'eard from Sam. I told 'er I 'adn't and yer know what she said? She said she 'opes we never see 'em agen! Then she insulted me about livin' off the Parish, even bragged about the two blokes 'er's livin' with, an' then she said I'd do betta not 'avin' another mouth to feed. I nearly throwed a plate at 'er – oh Hannah, I'm all shook up inside, will yer fetch me a drop of gin?'

'It ain't gin yer want, Polly, it's a good, strong bloody 'ot cuppa tea! Then yer can listen to what I goin' ter tell yer.'

'Is it good news? 'Cos if it ain't I don't wanta 'ear.'

'I think it will be good when yer 'ear it. Katie, put the kettle on the fire an' mek me an' yer mum a potta tea.' A pot of tea was often the beginning and end of any argument in our house. I was now all ears as I began to put the kettle on.

Granny sat facing Mum in the rocking chair and I heard her say, 'It's being Easter time, I went to the Mission, and as soon as all the people left I knelt down to pray for me son, an' fer the good Lord ter send 'im back once agen. The Captain saw me prayin' and asked me what me trouble was. When I told 'im we 'adn't 'eard from Sam fer several weeks, 'e kindly told me 'e would do what 'e could ter find 'im. Now, Polly, where's that first letter?'

'What yer want it for?' Mum asked suspiciously.

'I want it fer the address where 'e's workin!'

'I'll fetch it fer yer, Granny. It's on the shelf in Mum's bedroom.'

'Yer mum's quite capable of fetchin' it. You just mek that tea an' don't ferget ter warm the pot!'

I was expecting Mum to flare when Gran gave out her orders, but she just glared. As soon as she went upstairs, my granny started on me. 'What did I tell yer earlier terday?'

'What about, Granny?'

''Ow many more times 'ave I got ter tell yer *not* ter call me "Granny"?'

'But I've always called yer Granny!'

'Well, next time I want yer to call me Gran or Grandma, but never let me 'ear yer sayin' Granny agen!'

From that day forward I began to call her grandma. It sounded much nicer, and made me feel older.

Mum came down the stairs and handed the letter to Grandma.

'The Captain's gooin' ter post the letter to the Salvation Army in Manchester, explainin' why we're worried that Sam ain't bin answerin' Katie's letters. 'E said if anybody can find where 'e is, they can. But they need the address, so I'm mekin' it me business to find out where me son an' Bill Owens is lodgin'.'

'I ain't interested in Lizzie Owens' 'usband! Any'ow, where *yo* gooin' ter find the money ter goo all that bloody way to Manchester?'

'I've got a few shillings I put by for a rainy day. I can use some of that. Then there's me rent I can use, so that old skinflint can wait till I get back. But I ain't told the Captain any of this. Now, Katie,' she added, 'where's that cuppa tea I bin waitin' for?'

As I began to pour out the tea I asked Grandma if I could go with her, but she replied quickly, 'No, Katie. You've to attend school or they'll be mower trouble. Now, Polly. You'll be all right till I get back?'

'When yer gooin' then?'

'Tuesd'y mornin', an' I'll be stayin' at the Army in Manchester.'

'But who's gooin' ter feed yer cats?'

'I can go and feed them, Grandma,' I replied eagerly.

'No, luv! Me good neighbours will feed 'em. Any'ow,

you've gotta go ter school. An' yer won't be 'avin' yer babby yet, Polly.'

'But I'm still worried about the pains I keep getting,' Mum replied.

'Don't be such a fuss pot! Yo should know what they are by now after 'avin' all them kids! An' if Sam does come back yer wanta tell 'im ter pack 'is tool away.'

'Yo tell 'im! I've told 'im often enough. Any road, I don't expect any pity from yo!' she snapped.

I know Mum often made a lot of excuses about her troubles when she wanted attention, but my grandma never gave way to her. She was used to Mum's moans and groans.

Mary Makes Changes

Three days after my grandma left for Manchester, I came home from school at midday and was surprised to see smoke puffing from our chimney. It was always my job to light our fire on Wednesdays and Thursdays ready for when Mum came back from Green's and Sons Warehouse after taking the cards of linen buttons and hooks and eyes and collecting the few shillings she earned once a week.

When I got indoors I had a lovely surprise. Standing beside the fireplace was my eldest sister, Mary.

'Hello, Mary,' I cried out as I ran towards her. 'Have you come back home to stay?'

'I don't know yet, Katie. I haven't made my mind up, until I talk to Mum, anyway. Where is she?'

After I explained where she was, she replied, 'I've made a pot of tea so if you'll get a couple of cups and pour out, I'll try and explain why I'm here.' My sister was twelve years older than me and very pretty. Her lovely dark brown hair was bobbed and marcel-waved, the fashion then among young women.

As she bent down and kissed me, I couldn't help saying, 'You look lovely, Mary, and you smell so nice.'

'It's none of yer carbolic soap Mum uses. It's scented card I get from Snapes the chemist. It's called Phul-Nana.'

"Yer mean the one in Great Hampton Street?' I asked.

'That's the one. I call every Friday night after I get my wages and Mr Snapes gives me a card when I buy a tablet of Erasmic soap. I'm holding a club there now for the girls I work with, called a Diddleum Club.'

'What's that?' I asked.

'Well, twelve of us pay threepence a week for twelve weeks, twelve numbers go in the hat and each one picks out a number. As soon as their number comes out that's the week they can buy what they want. See what I mean?'

'It must be like when the "pat man" calls.'

'Yes,' she replied. 'Only I'm the pat man.' She smiled. 'Now, let's have another cup of tea before Mum gets back.'

No sooner had she said this than Mum walked in. The first thing she said when she saw Mary was, 'What yo doin' 'ere?'

'I've come to see how you're getting along, Mum, while Dad's away.'

'Yer know yer Dad's not 'ere an' I'm gooin' ter 'ave another babby!' Mum snapped.

'I can see that! Gran told me she was going to Manchester to make some enquiries about him.'

'Well, what brings yer 'ere now? Why dain't yer come 'afore yer dad left?' Mum asked.

'I didn't know anything about what's happened until Gran made it her business to come and tell me,' replied Mary.

''Ave yer come ter stop then?'

'That's what I've come to talk to you about. But first, if I should make my mind up and decide to come back, there are decisions to be made between us.'

I still remember that terrible night when Mary declared she was leaving home for good. She had come home late and Mum was waiting up for her. I was about to fall to sleep, when I heard them yelling at each other. I crept down the stairs to hear what it was all about, but Mum saw me and I made the excuse that I wanted to go to the lavatory.

'Well, 'urry yerself an' use the bucket next time,' she replied.

As I came back indoors I saw my sister weeping as she sat in Granny's rocker. I stood staring at her swollen lips until Mum cried out, 'Don't stand staring. Get yerself up to bed before yer get some an' all!' I knew then that Mum had beaten her.

I made my way towards the stairs but I didn't go back to bed; I wanted to know why mum had struck her. I sat quietly on the stairs and peeped through a crack in the door to see what it was all about. Suddenly Mum raised her voice again. 'I want the bloody truth or I'll give yer some mower!'

'I've told yer the truth! I've told yer! I missed the last tram from town,' Mary sobbed.

Mum hit her again. 'I don't believe yer! It don't tek 'alf an 'our ter walk from the terminus. An' yer can get yerself up ter bed!'

But before she rose from the chair I heard my dad come home. As soon as he saw Mary's face he cried out, 'What's been gooin' on, an' what's *she* done to yer?'

'She beat me, Dad, because she didn't believe I missed the tram.'

'Get ter bed, Mary. I'll settle this once and for all.'

'No, Dad. Now you're here you're going to hear what I have to say.'

'That's it! Yer can tell 'im wot yer like, I've got nothing ter be ashamed of,' Mum butted in.

'Neither have I! You've always been jealous of me, more so since I started courting, and I'm stopping the money out of me wages what you owe me!'

'What money is this?' Dad asked.

'She pawned my best coat, and when I asked her to fetch it out she said she hadn't got any money, so I had to get it myself. Anyway, as soon as I've collected my things together I'm leaving here for good!'

'If yer get in the family way don't come ter me for any pity, 'cause you'll get none! Mum replied bitterly.

'You've got Mary all wrong! She's got more sense in her little finger than you've got in yer 'ole body,' Dad yelled.

Suddenly Mum picked up a plate and threw it at him. As soon as he saw the blood he cried out, 'That's the last time you'll throw and get away with it!'

He struck Mum twice across the face, and as she screamed Dad went out, banging the door behind him. I knew it would be safer for me not to be seen, so I tiptoed back upstairs and got into bed beside Liza where I cried myself to sleep.

Next morning I was surprised that Liza hadn't heard the disturbance, and when I asked Frankie, he said, 'It don't bother me, they're always at it!' There was no sympathy from them two.

When Mary told Granny, there were more arguments and at the end of the week Mary packed her belongings and left home. I also knew that if my mum hadn't had such a bad temper or showed too many tantrums, my brothers Jack and Charlie would never have left home either.

After that terrible night my dad didn't come home for over a week. When he did, he told Mum he had stayed at the Rowton House. (This building is no longer for down and outs at a shilling a night; it is now a fashionable hotel.)

But now Mary was back, and she said to Mum, 'You better sit down and hear what I've got to say while Katie makes another pot of tea.'

'What yer mean another? I ain't got money ter waste buyin' tea! She can fill the pot with boiling water, I dare say it'll stand the strain. 'Ear what I say, Katie?'

'There you go agen, Mum. Always moanin' and snapping at her. She's been a little lackey for you, Mum,' Mary said.

'That's a lie. What's she bin tellin' yer?'

'She's told me nothing, I got eyes and ears! And I've known how she's put on. Anyway, where's Frankie and Liza? Why ain't they here to do their share?' Mary asked.

'They don't get 'ome till later. Four o'clock.'

'Why's that?' Mary asked.

'They 'ave ferther ter cum from Nelson Street school. Any'ow,' she added, 'where's that cuppa tea I'm waitin' for?'

'I've already poured it out, Mum,' I replied. 'It's on the table.'

As soon as she put the cup to her lips, it fell from her hand and she slumped on the floor holding her sides in pain. Mary and I bent over her as she lay groaning. Mary asked what was wrong.

'I've 'ad these pains fer four months. They keep comin' an' goin' an' each one gets worse.'

'Why don't yer see the doctor?' Mary asked.

'I ain't got money ter see the bloody doctor!' she yelled out as she doubled up again.

'Well, let me try to help you up,' Mary said.

Mum was a big weight, and as Mary and I tried to sit her up we saw blood run down her legs.

'Oh my God,' I cried out. 'What can we do, Mary? What has she cut herself with? We'll have to try and lift her up.'

But the more we tried to lift her the more Mum cried out. 'Just get me a drink of water, Mary, before I faint.'

I began to get frightened when I saw how pale she had gone, and as Mary put the cup of water to her lips she cried out, 'Not now, Mary, just try and get me up on the sofa and then I'll be all right. There's a drop of brandy on the shelf.'

'You'll *not* be all right! Water nor brandy will help you now. Anyhow, I'm calling in one of the neighbours to help me get you to bed.'

As Mum tried to sit up I saw the pool of blood. 'Oh, Mum! What have you done?' I cried out.

'Don't stand there staring,' Mary urged. 'Run and fetch one of the neighbours to help me!'

As I ran out of the house the only neighbour I saw was Mrs Owens, and I didn't know whether to tell her or not. I knew Mum didn't like her, but there was no one else handy because the rest of the neighbours were at the church for the Harvest Thanksgiving. There was nothing else for it but to ask Mrs Owens for help.

As we hurried indoors and Mum saw who I'd brought, she cried out, 'Who sent for yo?'

'No need ter trouble yerself, Polly, I've come ter 'elp!'

Mary and Mrs Owens lifted Mum on to the wooden sofa. Mum never said another word. I could see by now she was glad of the help, and as my sister gave her a sip of brandy, Mrs Owens said, 'I'm going for the doctor.'

'You'll fetch no doctor, I'll be all right when I've lay down for a while!'

'Well, you'll have to see somebody, Mum! Yer as white as a ghost. I'll slip up the street to see if Mrs Bullivant will see you.'

It wasn't long before Mary came back with the local midwife. Sarah Bullivant was a short, stocky, red-faced woman, who was always noted for her drops of gin. She was the only midwife for miles but attended only those women who could afford to pay; other women had to rely on friendly neighbours to help bring their babies into the world. But my sister Mary was worried and so paid for her to come.

As soon as she saw my mum she asked, 'How long has she been like this?'

'It 'appened about fifteen minutes agoo,' Mum managed to say.

'Well, we better get 'er upstairs an' into bed while you get the kettle on,' she said to me. 'I want plenty of hot water, paper and rags.'

She drew out a bottle from under her apron and took a long swill.

I had always been an inquisitive child, so while I waited for the kettle to boil I gathered all the waste paper I could find and sat on the stairs to listen. This was the only time in my life that I experienced my mum having a miscarriage, and learnt that everything was to be took away and burnt. Before the midwife left with her empty gin bottle she gave my sister instructions for Mum to stay in bed and rest, but if she got any worse Mary or Mrs Owens were to call the doctor in.

'Can't you give her anything to ease the pains?' Mary asked.

'I've nothing with me, but the doctor will know what ter do if you need him.'

As soon as Mrs Bullivant left Mary called Mrs Owens to one side and I heard her say, 'I think it will be for the best if I get the doctor *now*.'

But when Mum heard, she shouted, 'I ain't 'avin' no bleedin' quack maulin' me about. Just let me rest and I'll be all right termorra.' 'Tain't the first time I've 'ad a miss, but believe me, Mary, it'll be the last!' She cried out in pain.

'You've said that before, Mum,' Mary replied, 'and I hope you mean it this time. You're getting no younger and you're not out of danger yet. So drink this what Mrs Bullivant has left yer and rest. I'll be up agen as soon as I've given Frankie and Liza their orders, and if you want anything just bang on the floor.'

When Frankie and Liza came home from school the first thing they asked was, 'Where's Mum?'

'Yer Mum's not well. She's in bed and resting. Now I want you two to sit down and listen to what I say,' Mary told them. 'I've come back home to stay until yer mum gets better and you're to take orders from me!'

All at once Liza jumped up from her stool and made her way towards the stairs, but Mary was there before her.

'No, yer don't! Little madam! You'll stay where you are and listen to what I have to say, then you can have yer tea and then there's errands and jobs to be done.'

'Who sez so? I ain't tekin' no orders from *you*!' Liza exclaimed.

'You'll do as I say or else you'll get nothing to eat until yer do! That goes for you too, Frankie.'

'I do my whack, fetching the coal from the wharf, *and* I 'elp Katie, don't I, Katie?' Frankie piped up.

'Yes, you do, but Liza gets away with a lot. She's Mum's pet.' Mary added, 'There'll be no favouritism while I'm here. You've all got to do yer share, And you, Liza, I'm keeping my eye on you!'

Liza sat sulking the rest of the evening; Mary and I ignored her.

After washing up the supper dishes and putting everything in order for the morning, it was time for us to go to our bed in the attic. Mary said Mum was still fast asleep. We could peep in the room to see her on our way up, but we were not to wake her.

Next morning, after taking our orders from Mary, we went our separate ways, Frankie and Liza to Nelson Street and me to the school at the top of the hill. I was always home first, but Mary made it a rule that we had to have our tea together, then receive our orders. How different it was with Mary taking charge; although she spoke sharply, it was better than Mum bawling and clouting us, so we were happy to do as we were told. Although Liza grumbled at times, she soon learned that Mary was not to be ignored. Little did we know that that morning Mary had sent for Dr McKenzie and Mum had been taken by ambulance to Dudley Road infirmary.

News soon got around the district, but kind neighbours came each day to help in the brewhouse, hanging out the washing, and do other odd jobs. Mary went to see her boss and explained the circumstances and he told her she could do part-time until Mum was well again. Mary's young man came and helped out too.

Mum had only been in the infirmary three days when Grandma arrived back from her travels. As soon as Mary explained what had happened my grandma said, 'I

knew it would 'appen! I warned 'er not ter tek anythink
ter get rid of it an' now look what's 'appened!'

'But Mum told me she hadn't taken anything. She said
her pains had been coming and going for days!'

'I don't know what yer dad's gooin' ter say when 'e
'ears about this.'

'Where is he, Gran? When will he be here?' Mary
asked. 'I'm worn out trying to do my best and keep Liza
in check. She's a stubborn, cheeky little bugger at times.
I don't know how I keep my hands off her!'

'Yer dad'll soon tek 'er in 'and when 'e comes back
'ome,' Grandma said.

'But *when's* he coming, Gran?' Mary repeated.

'The end of the week, so 'e said.'

'How did yer come to find him?'

'Not in bloody Manchester! That was a waste of time
and money. Stayin' nights at the Salvation Army
Mission – it gave me the creeps! I was afeared ter get ter
sleep, what with all the down an' outs comin' an' gooin'.
I was glad when the Captain came one mornin' and told
me my son was workin' in Birmingham as a porter on the
Great Western Railway.'

'Why, that's only about a mile from here! I wonder
why he 'ain't been back home ter see us?'

'I ain't got time ter explain, Mary, but 'e'll tell yer in 'is
own way when 'e gets 'ere. Now, luv,' she added, 'mek
me a nice strong cuppa tea. I ain't 'ad a decent one since
I left 'ere. Then I'll 'ave ter goo 'ome and see what's bin
gooin' on while I've bin away.'

'No need ter worry, Gran. I've bin up there and given
your house a good spring clean. I've also seen to the cats,

but the landlord called and said you owed three weeks' rent and if you don't pay up within a few days he'll be giving notice to quit. I would have paid some of it for yer but I couldn't afford to.'

'Why, the bloody old skinflint! 'E can wait a bit longer. Any'ow, it's two weeks not three! But thank yer, luv,' she added. 'Yer a good wench. I only wish all mothers 'ad daughters like you. Ta ta fer now, an' let me know when yer dad comes 'ome.'

'I will, Gran. Look after yourself and thanks for helping ter find me dad,' said Mary.

Friday night was our bath night. My job had always been to fetch in the zinc bath from the wall outside the house and to take the iron kettle down to the tap in the yard, then bring it back ready to put on the coal fire to heat up the water. But as soon as I got outside to reach for the bath to drag it inside I heard Mary call out, 'Not you, Katie. That'll be Frankie's job from now on.'

'I don't mind, Mary,' came Frankie's reply.

'Very well then,' she said. 'Liza can take the kettle and fill it, and you, Katie, can help me sort out yer clean shifts.'

Liza jumped up. 'That kettle's too heavy for me ter carry! Any'ow, that's always been Katie's job.'

'Well, it's your job from now on and it's no use yer sulking. Move yerself!' Mary replied.

As she snatched the kettle from the hob Liza threatened, 'You wait, our Mary, till Mum comes 'ome. You'll find a difference then, who's who and what's what, yer bloody bossy cow!'

Mary glared at her. She couldn't believe her ears, but she didn't say anything until Liza returned with the kettle of water.

As she took the kettle, Mary asked very calmly, 'What did you call me?'

Liza turned her head away without answering.

'Did you hear what I said?' Mary asked.

Still Liza didn't answer.

'Very well. If you don't want to answer me I'm going to force your mouth open and pour the water from this kettle down your throat. For the last time, you'll either say you didn't mean it or answer me!'

Frankie and I looked on, wondering if Mary was going to carry out her threat. Then, as she turned to place the kettle on the fire, Liza put her tongue out and said, 'Well, you *are* a bloody bossy cow!'

Mary didn't answer her, but turning to Frankie she said, 'Frankie, you don't want to see your sisters undressing and taking their bath. Here's a penny. Take a piece of soap and a towel and take yerself off to Northwood Street Baths.'

As Frankie moved towards the door he winked and grinned at me. We both knew Liza would get her come-uppance now.

As soon as he closed the door behind him Liza began to undress, and as she stood naked beside the bath waiting for the hot water, Mary called out, 'Come on, get in, I'm not waiting for you all night!'

'But I'm waitin' for yer to put some hot water in.'

'A little cold bath won't hurt yer. *Now, get in!*' Mary ordered.

'No! No! I ain't getting in for you nor anybody else, till yer pour some hot water in!' Liza yelled.

'You'll have more than hot water before I'm through with yer! Now are you going to get in?'

'No! No I ain't, and you can't make me!'

Suddenly Mary picked her up, dropped her into the cold water and held her down. As she began to yell and splutter, Mary washed her mouth out with the carbolic soap. Her screams could be heard all over the neighbourhood, but no one seemed to notice or wonder why; the neighbours were used to the noise of everyday life.

When Liza stopped yelling, she was told to get washed, especially behind her ears. When the kettle boiled Mary then poured some into the bath. As soon as Liza had finished she stepped out and began drying herself in front of the fire, crying.

'No use yer blartin' now! Perhaps that'll teach you a lesson not to swear and call me names. Now, when you've get yer shift on, you can help me and Katie to drag the bath outside and empty it down the drain.'

'What about *her* bath?' Liza cried out, pointing at me.

'Katie will have some fresh water, *not* what you've piddled in.'

'I dain't piddle in it!'

'Don't tell me any more lies. I saw the bubbles rising, and heard 'em!'

Liza was given her drink of cocoa and told to get up to bed. As she got halfway up the stairs she called out, 'You wait till Mum hears about this, yer bossy bloody . . .' Before she could finish, Mary flew up after her and slapped her bare bottom hard several times before Liza could reach the attic.

As Mary came back into the room I said, 'Mary, I hope she don't take her revenge out on me when I go up.'

'You just let *me* know and she'll get more than she got tonight. And that was only a taste of what she *will* get if she tells Mum or Dad.'

'Dad never takes any notice of her now,' I said.

'Why's that?'

'Because Mum can't see any wrong in her and Dad loses his patience and then they start to quarrel.'

'Well, Katie, from now on, while I'm here, there's going to be a few changes. Now come and get in while the water's warm before yer brother comes back.' As she began to wash my hair she asked when I'd had it cut short.

'Mum cut if off when I had nits.'

How gentle she was as she rubbed my back; how different it was from my mother's impatient handling and slapping. I dried myself with our rough hessian towel, put on my clean calico shift, and after drinking a cup of hot cocoa, I was ready for bed.

I was more than pleased to see that Liza was fast asleep as I crept in beside her. I lay awake for a long time hoping and praying that our lives would be different now that Mary had come back. Before I fell asleep, I remembered the time when my mum cut all my lovely long dark hair off. Liza always wore her hair tied back with real ribbon, but mine had been two short plaits tied back with a piece of string.

As there were no gardens to our back-to-back

houses, I often found pleasure walking through Key Hill and Warstone Lane Cemetery, where I would take out my pencil and paper and write down some of the epitaphs from the tombstones, and smell the lovely wreaths of flowers. One day I happened to look up and see my sister Liza. I noticed at once that she wore a fresh bow of pink ribbon in her hair. When I asked where she'd got it from she replied, 'You've seen it before, why ask?'

I knew she was lying. 'You didn't have that this morning, you had blue on,' I pointed out.

'Well, if yer want to know, it was lying among some dead flowers and a heap of rubbish. There's some more if you want one.'

'Are you sure you haven't took it from one of the graves?'

'No, I ain't!' she replied. 'If yer come with me I'll show yer!'

Around the back of a wall there were several piles of grass cuttings and dead flowers, but I couldn't see any ribbons until Liza began to dig it over. Sure enough, beneath the rubbish were several pieces of coloured ribbons, but they were covered in mud, not fresh like the piece Liza wore. I wondered if she *had* taken it from one of the wreaths. I was about to ask her when she told me to hurry before the gravedigger found us.

'But it belongs to the people buried here,' I objected.

'Well, they don't want it! Take what you want before the keeper comes to lock the gates,' she said. 'Anyway, I've heard said that the gypsies come when it's dark and help themselves.'

Although I had a feeling it was wrong, I couldn't resist helping myself to a piece of scarlet ribbon.

As soon as I got home I washed it, and when it was dry I hid it where no one would see it or know where I had got it from, only Liza and she swore she would never divulge our secret. I only wore it when I went to Band of Hope and Sunday School, then before going home I would take it off and hide it away. I loved and treasured that piece of ribbon.

Then one Sunday I forgot to take it off and Mum saw it. 'Where 'ave yer got that from? she shouted.

I knew she would find out if I told a lie, but when I told her the truth she yelled, 'Yer need ter goo ter Sunday School, yer wicked devil! And whoever it belonged to, I 'ope they come ter 'aunt yer!'

Suddenly she got the scissors and cut my two plaits off and threw them on the fire, then slapped my face hard. I've never forgotten the awful smell of that ribbon and my two plaits as I watched them burning.

I often wondered if my mum ever knew or asked where Liza got her different ribbons from. I could have told her but I knew she wouldn't believe me. In any case, I didn't want to suffer at the hands of Liza. After that I never trusted or believed in my sister again.

Breakfast with my eldest sister looking after us was toast or Quaker Oats. I knew she used most of her wages and a few shillings from Albert, her young man, to pay the rent and feed us. My brothers Jack and Charlie were not living at home, and neither had been to see us since they had moved out. Some weeks when Mum happened to meet my brother Charlie, he would give her a few shillings, but Jack was on the dole or so he made out when he happened to bump into her. I remember he was always selfish and tight-fisted.

Liza, Frankie and I were always grateful for our school breakfast, which consisted of two thick slices of bread and jam, and an enamel mug of hot cocoa, winter and summer. It was no wonder there was always regular attendance at school.

Finding Mum's Treasure

One afternoon, I hurried home to tell my sister that all us older girls were given four days' holiday. 'We've been told by the Vicar that all us older girls have to leave,' I explained excitedly.

'Well, you better sit down and tell me the reason before the other two get home, or you'll have Liza twisting your story,' Mary said.

'It's not a story, Mary, it's true! The Vicar came this afternoon and gave all us girls a lecture and explained that now he intends to keep our mixed church school for "my boys" only, as he calls them. Starting next Monday morning, all girls are to be transferred to another school in Spencer Street, in the Jewellery Quarter.'

'Do yer think you'll like the change?' she asked.

'Yes, I'm pleased really. I shall still be with my friends, and what's better still our same teachers will be coming too. It's all been arranged and we've been given our orders, the girls have to help carry books and ledgers and whatever other necessities.'

'But why can't some of the lads help?' Mary asked.

'Oh no, Mary! The Vicar was adamant and said it was a job for the girls to do. Anyway, he keeps a watchful eye on his boys since that last incident,' I explained.

'Oh, you mean when Frankie was punished?'

'It wasn't his fault he was dismissed from school. It was that cheeky lad Billy Aspley who lives in Graham Street. He was the one who should have been caned and dismissed.'

'It's the first I've heard. I think you'd better tell me the whole story.'

I sat down on one of our backless chairs and began. 'I know why us girls are really being transferred to another school. There's been a lot of trouble between the boys and the girls, and neither the Vicar nor the headmaster like us mixing any more.'

'Yes,' Mary said,' I did hear something, but you know how gossip flows from one mouth to another.'

'This wasn't gossip. The truth is I was there and saw it happen, and when I tried to explain to the master and the Vicar I was punished with the cane too.'

'Well, I'd like to know what really happened.'

'Well, Mary, girls and boys only mixed together for our exercises in the playground and always under the eye of Mr Holland, the headmaster. Often, some of the boys would tease the girls when the master wasn't looking. One afternoon I saw Maggie Bowens plaiting her legs, and when I asked her if she wanted the lavatory she said someone was already in there. I told her to go into the boys and I'd look out for her. She went in and closed the door and I stood outside to keep watch, but Frankie and two other boys saw me and asked what Maggie was doing in there. I told them she couldn't wait and that she had already wet herself.

'"Well, she'd better hurry up out of there before the Master sees her",' Frankie said.

'Billy Aspley was grinning all over his face. "Let's go in and tease 'er!" he said.

'"No yer don't or I'll get the master!" I yelled. But before I could say another word Billy pushed me away and the next thing I knew he pushed Frankie inside and held the door shut. Before Frankie could realise what had happened the headmaster came bounding across the yard. Frankie, Maggie and me were marched back into the classroom, but the master didn't wait for us to explain. Maggie and me were sent into another room where we had several lashes from the bamboo cane, but Frankie had to drop his trousers in front of the other boys in his class, who all saw the master beating him on his bare bottom.'

'Wasn't the Aspley lad punished?' Mary asked.

'No, but Frankie swore he'd get his own back, and one dark night he saw Billy whistling away with his hands in his pockets. Frankie left him with a bleeding mouth and a tooth missing. Billy never told anyone what really happened, only that he had walked into a lamp-post.'

'Yes, Frankie'll take care of bullies if they take him on. Now, Katie, put the kettle on and we'll have a cup of tea and a piece of my home-made cake before the other two get home.'

'I know Liza will be jealous and want to know the whys and wherefores, but I shall only tell her I'm going to a girls' school in Spencer Street. She can find out the rest for herself,' I added.

Frankie was pleased to hear the news, but as expected I only got the usual sulks and grumbles from Liza. The next morning after they had left for school Mary asked me if I would help around the house with the cleaning and washing. 'You know I will, Mary,' I replied.

'Gran called last night and told me she'd seen our dad and he's coming home in a day or two. I'd like to get this place a bit ship-shape before he gets here, but would you rather go to the park with your friends?'

'I can go another time, Mary,' I replied.

'Well, we'll have our breakfast, then we'll think about what's to be done first.'

I knew Mary sometimes had a couple of slices of bacon or scrambled eggs for her breakfast, and this morning, instead of my usual porridge and toast, she made me sit down at the table with her to a rasher of bacon, a fried egg and fried bread. After eating it and drinking another cup of tea from the only two cups Mum owned with handles, I filled the two iron kettles from the tap in the yard and kept my sister well supplied with hot water from the coal fire, while she was upstairs stripping beds.

My job was to scrub the wooden table, two wooden backless chairs, one ladderback chair and the wooden sofa with disinfectant and carbolic soap. I was in the middle of my chores when I heard Mary call at the top of her voice, 'Katie! Come up at once!' I hurried up to the attic. 'Katie, is this where you and Liza sleep?'

'Yes, and Frankie,' I replied.

'You mean to say Frankie sleeps in the same bed as you and Liza?'

'Frankie don't sleep with us, Mary, he sleeps at the foot of the bed.'

'Well, from now on he'll sleep in Jack's bed in Mum's bedroom. Now where's your sheets and blankets?'

'We ain't got any, only one blanket and Dad's old Army coat. Mum pawned them and she never fetched them out again.'

I had never seen Mary so angry. 'Do you know where she keeps the pawn tickets?' she demanded.

'In the vase on the mantel-shelf,' I said.

'Well, we'll leave what we're doing and sort them out.'

We had to sort through several before we came across what we were looking for. There was a ticket for an alarm clock, brass fire irons, an old gramophone, and several others that it was now too late to redeem.

'You can come with me to the pawn shop,' Mary said.

'But where's the money to come from?' I asked.

'I'm going to use the money yer mum left on the shelf for the rent,' Mary replied.

'But the landlord has promised the bailiffs if she don't pay, and I know she's still behind,' I protested.

'Another week won't hurt. I'll pay him out of my wages at the end of the week, unless Dad's got a few bob. Don't look so worried! You leave the worrying to me. Yer mum won't have it all her own way now I've come back home.'

'But she'll go mad when she finds out you've used the rent money.'

'She'll change her tune when she finds out I'm taking over,' she said as she kissed my cheek and stroked my hair. 'Honestly, don't look so worried. Let's see yer smile, because from now on there will be no more beatings if I have anything to do with it. Now, we'll have another cuppa before we fetch the bundles out.'

As we came out of the pawn shop with the bundles under our arms, we saw Mrs Owens. 'Hello, Mary, how's yer mum?'

'Just comfortable,' Mary replied.

''Ave yer been ter see 'er yet?'

'No, I don't have the time, but that's what I'm told when I phone the post office, and believe me, Mrs Owens, I ain't looking forward to her coming home!' Mary said.

'But perhaps she'll be better tempered when yer dad comes home.'

'How did you know, I only heard myself last night?' Mary asked.

'I met yer gran coming out of the Mission and she told me.'

'By the way, Mrs Owens, I haven't thanked you for helping me. You must come and have a cup of tea with me one of these afternoons.'

'But what if yer mum's there?' she asked.

'She's got to thank you too! I think she would have died if you hadn't been there to help me that night.'

'Think nothing of it, love. If I can't do a good turn it's not me, but thank you, Mary, for talking to me. It's more than any of me neighbours do since I come to live with George and his brother, Ted. Maybe we could get together sometime, if you're interested. You see, I've never talked to anyone about myself before, but I'd like you to hear my story.'

'Yes, I think I'd like to know why the neighbours dislike you, but I know some of them need to ask *themselves* questions,' Mary answered.

'I don't care what they think – I'm not the only pebble on the beach living in sin.'

'Don't say any more in front of Katie.'

'I'm sorry, Mary, I wasn't thinking. But why ain't she in school?'

'She's moving to a new school soon. Now I really must go, I've a lot ter do before Dad gets home.'

We hurried away, and as soon as we arrived home we unwrapped the dusty pieces of rag from around the bundles. Out fell well-patched sheets and blankets. They looked grubby and faded, but Mary set to right away, dropping them into a bath of disinfectant and soapy water. As soon as they were ready to be put through the mangle I helped her and then we pegged them out on the line across the yard.

'There's a good wind, and if the sun keeps out they'll be dry soon,' said Mary. 'If not we'll place 'em on the fire guard and stoke the fire up.'

When we came back indoors, Mary said she needed me upstairs again to help disinfect the iron bedsteads, the laths, and to spray our flock mattress with Keatings powder. She also worked very hard on her bed, which had not been used since she left home. Her trunk still lay locked up on the other side of the attic, and we knew it contained her bed linen and other articles she was putting to one side for when she married. I often used to hear her say it was her 'bottom drawer'.

When Frankie and Liza got home I helped Mary serve up the rabbit stew and dumplings for dinner, and after they went back to school in the afternoon, we went to the Rag Market to see if we could spot some bargains. Mary bought some lace curtains and some American oil cloth to hide the stains on our table, as well as some pillow slips for our bed.

After she bought some stewing meat and a rabbit from the open-air meat market, she led me into Lyons Corner House for a cup of coffee and a cream horn. Oh how I wished that day could occur regularly.

It was ten minutes to four o'clock when we arrived home. Everything was neat and tidy and in its place. As Mary toasted muffins by the fire I began to cut and margarine the bread ready for us all to sit down together and have our tea, when Liza and Frankie came in.

Liza immediately sniffed and asked, 'What's that smell? It smells like a hospital in here!'

'Yes, it does!' Frankie agreed. 'What is it, Mary?'

'Never mind if yer don't know, yer'll soon find out!' Mary replied. 'And you, Liza, can hang that coat up. I'm not having you throwing your coat on the sofa.'

'Where I gotta hang it then?' she snapped.

'Plenty of nails on the pantry door. Then you can both wash your hands and sit up to the table and get yer tea. Let me remind you both that while I'm here I'm not having you grabbing a slice of bread and running outside with it. Do you both understand?'

'Yes,' Frankie said, but Liza only nodded.

'I didn't hear any answer from you, Liza,' Mary commented.

Suddenly Liza spat, 'Hark at Miss Gobby Chops agen!' In a flash Mary sprang out of her chair and as she began to shake Liza she shouted, 'If I have any more nasty remarks from *you* I'll tan yer bloody bare arse with Dad's razor strap! Now sit down and get yer tea.'

But Liza still stood glaring. I was afraid now in case she said another word. 'She means it, Liza, so yer better not answer her back.'

'Who asked you ter pipe up!' Liza retorted.

'Shut yer gob, Liza, and sit down!' Frankie yelled, as he pushed her roughly on to the chair.

Our tea was then eaten in silence.

When we'd finished, Mary told Liza to take the bucket and fetch some coal from the cellar.

'I ain't goin' down no cellar, that's Frankie's job.'

"I'll go,' Frankie replied at once.

'No, you won't,' Mary interrupted. 'She'll do as she's told or she'll know what to expect. And you, Frankie, can fill me the brewhouse boiler ready for tomorrow's wash.'

I saw him willingly pick up the bucket which he began swinging around, and heard him whistling that same old ditty he taught me called 'That Little Shirt Me Muvver Made For Me'. Often, when we were asked to sing at school parties, Frankie and I would sing it together.

As soon as my brother was out of sight Liza piped up again sarcastically, 'What's yer favourite sister's chores then?'

'I have no favourites,' Mary said, 'but let me tell you, Katie's been fetching and carrying and helping me to give the beds and bedrooms a good clean, when she could have gone to the park with her school friends. Perhaps you'd like to change jobs with her?' she added.

There was no answer, only more shrugs.

'And while I'm on the subject, when you've finished your jobs I might let you go out to play, but I don't want any of the neighbours complaining about you chalking outside their doors.'

'It wasn't me!'

'I don't want any more of your lies, you were seen!'

When Liza emerged from the cellar with the bucket of rough slack and coal, Mary said she had to take the oil can and fetch a pint of paraffin, 'And be quick about it before it gets dark. Here's the threepenny bit and *don't* lose it!'

I was surprised to see she went without another grumble.

As soon as she was gone Mary pulled down the hanging lamp from the ceiling, and whilst she trimmed the wick and I washed the glass chimney I heard her mutter, 'I'll tame that cheeky brazen bugger if it's the last thing I do.'

But I knew that was going to be easier said than done.

Two days later, just after Frankie and Liza had left for school, the door was suddenly flung open and in walked our dad. Mary and I could not believe our eyes. He was so different from when he left with Bill Owens to find work in Manchester; he looked much older and thinner, and was unshaven with a dark grey beard. He was still wearing the shabby grey cap my brother Jack had often teased him about, and the same old suit, now well worn since he'd left home.

His first greeting was for Mary. 'Hello, Mary, love, what brings you here?'

'I've come to stay, Dad,' she replied.

They threw their arms around each other and it was then that he noticed me. He picked me up in his arms, and as he hugged and kissed me he asked why I wasn't in school.

'I've got ter go to Spencer Street Girls School now, Dad,' I explained. 'Our Vicar wants our church school to be for boys only.'

When he had put me down he asked, 'Where's yer mum?'

'Don't yer know?' Mary replied.

'Know what?'

'Mum's in Dudley Road Hospital, Dad. Didn't Gran tell yer?'

'No, luv. Yer gran only said I was needed at home. Anyway, what's happened, has she had an accident?'

'She had a bad miscarriage and was taken away in an ambulance.'

'But why didn't you let me know? I would have come home sooner. Anyway, I didn't even know she was pregnant agen.'

'How could any of us let yer know? We didn't know where you were until Gran got in touch with the Salvation Army. Anyhow, she's on the mend now and Gran says she'll be back home in a few days. Is it true you're working as some kind of porter on Snow Hill

Station? Surely you could have come home and stopped us all worrying. Mum even thought you'd gone off with another woman.'

'She would think that,' he replied, smiling. 'It's a long story, love. I'll explain when I get back from seeing yer mum.'

'But yer carn't go in that state, Dad. Yer look like a tramp! You'd better have a wash and shave, and if yer go upstairs and throw yer clothes down I'll brush and press them, then you'll look more presentable.'

As Dad's clothes came flying down the stairs, Mary asked, 'Where's Mum's iron, I hope she ain't got it pawned now!'

'It's on the pantry shelf, Mary.' I picked up Dad's clothes and handed them over to her.

'Very well, I'll get it. You slip up to the attic and throw the blanket down off yer bed.'

As I reached the first landing I heard Dad call, 'Who's there?'

'It's only me, Katie. I'm going up to the attic to fetch our Mary a blanket to press yer clothes on.'

When I came back down I saw Mary standing on the step giving Dad's clothes a good shake, inside and out. We noticed Mrs Owens making her way to our house. 'I hear yer dad's come home, Mary.'

'Yes, he's upstairs changing.'

'Do you mind if I come in and have a word with him?'

'I'm sure I don't know, what's it all about?' asked Mary.

'I only want ter know if 'e knows where my husband's stayin'.'

'Just wait there and I'll have a word with him.'

'Mary,' I whispered, 'I don't think you better call her in, you know me dad don't like her.'

'She ain't so bad as people paint her,' said Mary. 'And I can already see Sarah Ford and her two cronies straining their necks to see what's going on. Now you put the iron in the fire and I'll call her in. ' She stuck her head outside. 'Come on in and sit down, Mrs Owens, if yer don't mind waiting while I press his clothes. But I hope you won't keep him long, he's eager to visit me mum,' Mary told her.

As soon as Mrs Owens sat down she looked straight at me. 'I know yer dad don't like me (Had she heard what I had said?), but I've got ter know where my husband is. It's urgent.'

I handed Mary the hot iron from between the bars and we watched as she began to press Dad's trousers. When they were finished I took them up to his room, and as I pushed them through the narrow gap in the door I heard Mary and Mrs Owens whispering together.

Dad came downstairs, and as soon as he saw Mrs Owens sitting there, he shouted, 'What's *she* doing here?'

'She just wants a few words with you, Dad,' Mary replied.

'I've nothing to say ter that woman, and yer mum will go mad when she finds out she's been here. Just tell her to go.'

Mrs Owens got up to leave and I saw tears in her eyes. Suddenly Mary cried, 'You'll stay where you are.' She faced Dad and said, 'You listen to *me*! I know you say you don't like her, but she's not so bad as people paint her. She's really got her heart in the right place, and let me tell you *this*. Mum wouldn't be alive today if it hadn't been for Mrs Owens' help! Now I think you owe her an apology and to listen to what she has to say.'

'I ain't got the time. Yer know I have ter visit yer mum.'

'There's plenty of time. You don't have to leave till two o'clock. Surely you can spare a few minutes. Come on, Dad, you can see she's upset by what you've said.'

Mrs Owens began, 'I wanted to ask if you could tell me where Bill is living or working.'

'I'm sorry if I've upset you, Mrs Owens. I'm afraid I don't know where your husband is living or working now, but why do you want to know?' Dad asked.

'The police are looking for him to serve a summons for maintenance, and I thought you might know as you both went to work on a building site in Manchester together.'

'All I can tell you is we was led up the garden path with that job. We were promised a good wage and a permanent job, but after a couple of weeks it was finished. Bill stole some tools, said he was going to start on his own, but I never trusted him and when the boss found out there was this awful fight. Bill struck out several times with the shovel, nearly killed the bloke, and when the police came they arrested him. He may still be in jail for all I know.'

'Is that all you can tell me, Sam?'

'I'm afraid so, but I do know he was living with a woman in a back street, I think it was called Conimoor Street or Colimore Street, something like that. It was near where he was working when he was arrested. I know he came to see me at my lodgings when he was out on bail, but I didn't see him. My landlady said he left a message saying he would kill me if I gave evidence, so I thought it was best for me to find other lodgings. The only help I could get was from the Salvation Army. They fed me and gave me night shelter for selling their leaflets the *War Cry* and *Little Soldier*. I am afraid that's all I can tell you. Anyway,' he added, 'you ain't come here to hear my troubles.'

'Well, wherever he is, or whatever kind of woman 'e's with, she's welcome to 'im. I hope when the police catch up with 'im they hand 'im in,' she replied bitterly.

'Put the kettle on, Katie. I'm sure Mrs Owens could do with a cup of tea,' Dad said.

'Thanks all the same, but my lodgers will be home soon. Perhaps I can come agen when yer wife gets home?'

'I'm sorry for those harsh words. I know my wife will thank you too for your kindness. Now I must hurry, but I'll let you know how she's faring,' he added, as he kissed Mary and me and left.

No one wanted any tea now so I took the kettle off the fire and placed it singing on the hob while my sister went upstairs to tidy the bedroom.

It was the middle of March, a wet, bitterly cold, windy day, and as I sat by the fire warming my feet I began to think over what my dad had said. That was why his letters had ceased to arrive along with the allowance to Mum, but he could have written to me and explained. Perhaps he thought I was too young to understand or he didn't want Mum to worry. Anyway, I was happy to know he was home again and I hoped Mum would be happy too and forgive him when she heard his story, for all our sakes.

When Mary came downstairs, she said, 'It's bloody freezing up there. As soon as I get a bit of money to spare I'll get Dad ter put a couple of panes in, and that sash cord in the attic wants mending too. Now let's get the table laid, Katie, and a good fire burning for when yer dad gets back.'

As I began to poke the dead ashes from the bottom fire bars, I noticed the ash pan was full. 'Mary, I think the ash pan needs to be emptied.'

'When was it last done?' she asked.

'I don't know. Mum never let any of us do it, she always did it herself.'

'All right, let me see to it before any more ash falls.'

She got on her knees and I handed her the bucket and shovel. As she began to shovel the ash, out came a Cadbury's Cocoa tin.

'What's this doing here?' She held the tin up for me to see and shook it. 'Sounds like money.' She blew the dust off and removed the lid and we were surprised to see half-crowns, two shilling pieces, sixpences, silver three-penny bits, a few pennies and some farthings roll out.

'Well, I wonder who's hid this here?' Mary said.

'None of us are allowed to empty that well, only Mum. I only know that the last time I emptied it was a long time ago, and when she told me *she* would do the job in future I was glad, as when I emptied it into the miskin on a windy day all the dust blew back on me.'

'So it must be Mum's then. Well, well! The crafty old

sod.' Mary smiled. 'So that's where she hides the money, and 'er always saying she can't make ends meet!'

'You'd better put it back where yer found it, Mary, or there'll be hell to pay. Yer know what Mum's like.'

'I'll do nothing of the sort!' she exclaimed.

'But she's sure to blame me, I know she will.'

'No, she won't, and don't look so worried! Listen to what I'm going to do, I'm going to keep it somewhere safe for the time being and when Mum comes home again I'm going to enjoy watching her when she next empties the ashes. I don't want you to say a word about this to anyone, and I want you to be with me. Now promise and let's see you smile again.'

I tried hard not to look worried as I promised.

We had tidied up the hearth and were washing our hands in a bowl of warm water when we heard someone banging on the door.

'See who that is, Katie. If it's Mrs Owens tell her I'm too busy ter see her now, an' ter call later.'

I opened the door. 'It's the agent for the rent, Mary.' But before I could say another word, he pushed past me almost knocking me over.

'You tell yer dad I want some rent and some arrears terday or else!' he yelled.

'Me dad ain't here. He's gone ter visit me mum in hospital!' I replied.

'You'll have ter wait and there's no use yer yellin'. You heard what my sister said. Anyway, you'll get it at the end of the week!' Mary told him.

'See that I do. I'm fed up with the promises from bad tenants around this district, so I'm warning yer parents for the last time!' After clearing his throat he left, banging the door behind him.

'Come here, Katie. Don't look so worried, everything will turn out right in the end. Let's put another lump on the fire before yer dad comes,' said Mary.

Everything was ship-shape again and the kettle already simmering when Dad came in shivering and wet through. As he took his wet clothes off and sat down by the fire I asked him how Mum was.

'The doctor said she could have been discharged yesterday but she's giving the nurses a lot of trouble.'

'I'm not surprised, and what kind of trouble is that?' asked Mary.

'It seems they're having trouble getting her bowels open. She refused to use the bed pan, and during the night she got out of bed to go to the lavatory and fell. It seems some of the other patients told the sister that yer mum is always getting out of bed to go to the lavatory in the night. Now she's to be kept in bed for a few more days with the use of a bed pan, and the doctor tells me that if she gets out of bed again without using the pan he'll have her strapped down!'

'Oh, Dad, how cruel! Can they really do that?' I asked.

'You'd be surprised what these hospitals can do if yer stubborn and don't take their orders.'

'I can't see why she' so fussy,' Mary chipped in. 'A bed pan – why it's better than sitting on a bucket!'

'I know,' Dad replied. 'I'll get me a couple of pots as soon as I start work.'

'Have you anything in mind, Dad?' Mary asked.

'Yes, luv. I was about to break the good news but there wasn't time when I heard yer mum was in hospital. Now, if you'll both draw yer chairs up to the fire, I'll tell yer about it, and how it happened.'

I was all ears as we sat either side of him.

'Before I begin,' he said, 'has Jack or Charlie been ter visit yer mum?'

'I believe Charlie has, Dad,' I replied. 'But I know that Jack hasn't.'

'Jack couldn't care less!' Mary added.

'I know, I know,' Dad repeated, shaking his head. 'And how's Frankie and Liza?'

'Frankie's been a good help,' Mary replied, 'but I've got me work cut out with that cheeky bugger. She swears and tells lies, and when I tell her to get in the bath she swears at me calling me a "bloody bossy old cow!" I rubbed carbolic soap on her tongue, but I don't think that'll cure her!'

'I gave up trying a long time ago, Mary. Yer mum never did listen to me when I found her stealing food from the cupboard and blaming it on somebody else. I know she causes a lot of arguments in the home, but maybe she'll grow out of her selfish ways as she gets older.'

'Well, I've come back home to stay, Dad, and from now on I'd like your permission to take her in hand.'

'You do what you think's best, luv. But remember you'll have yer mum against yer at times.'

'I've already spoken to her before she went into hospital.'

'And what did she say?' Dad asked.

'She agreed on condition that I came home to stay.'

'Well, don't upset yer mum too much. I know she has a vile temper at times, but she's had a lot to put up with over the years, and not being able to read and write don't help, although God knows I've tried to teach her. I know you'll do your best, Mary.'

'I intend to, Dad,' she replied. 'Now what's this you're going to tell us about a job?'

Although I was never allowed to butt in unless spoken to, I was listening and taking it all in, hoping that what I was about to hear would change our lives for the better, and hoping Mum would change too.

Looking For Work

'I was very grateful for all the kindness I received from the Salvation Army, but I still had my pride, Mary,' Dad began. 'I had to make my way back to Brum and find work here somehow. You must understand how desperate I was without a penny in my pocket, hitch-hiking and sleeping rough until I arrived in Snow Hill. That's when I found myself relying on tips for carrying people's luggage. It was the only job I could get with so many people out of work. Some people were generous, but others just raised their hats without even a thank you. I thank the good Lord that I won't be doing that job agen!'

'Well, Dad, what have you got in mind? Mum is sure to expect you to find some money. You know how she is when there's little coming in from public assistance, and what I can afford ain't much.'

'I can see you are doing your best and I thank you for

everything. Now it's time to repay you, and it'll be sooner than you all expect.'

'Why?' Mary replied, smiling. 'Are you thinking of robbing a bank?'

'No, nothing like that, luv. I've been offered a job in a factory and it *will* be permanent this time.'

'Are you sure, Dad! Where and who with?' I cried out excitedly.

'Let's have another cuppa and then you can both hear about it.'

As soon as we had settled down again, Dad began to tell his story.

'A little while ago, I happened to be carrying three heavy cases for a real toff who gave me a silver shilling. I raised my cap as usual and thanked him. Each day after that he alighted from the train and looked along the platform for *me*. There were always others whom he could have called out to, but it seemed he always wanted me. Then one morning he asked me to carry two portmanteaux and a portfolio to a waiting cab. As I put them inside, he took off his kid gloves and gave me a half-crown. As the cab drove away, I noticed he had dropped his wallet. I picked it up quickly but the cab was out of sight. I was afraid someone would come along and think I'd stolen it and I thought of taking it to the Police Station in Kenyon Street, but I had my doubts as to whether they would keep it so I hid it under my waistcoat. When I got to Rowton House where I was sleeping nights, I opened it to find an address where I could contact the owner. Believe me, Mary, my eyes nearly popped out of my head. I'd never seen so much money in my life. I didn't know what to do.'

'But you didn't keep it did you, Dad?' I asked.

'No! But believe me, Katie, I was tempted. When I looked at the back of the wallet I found his name and address on a gilt-edged card. Also a small faded photo of a grey-haired old lady who could have been his mother or some other relative.

'I closed the wallet quickly before the other men saw; I wouldn't be alive today if they had got wind of what I had hidden. That night I was afraid even to shut my eyes.

'Next morning, just as it began to get light enough for me to see, I crept along the dark passage fully dressed and then out into the street. As I passed many, many traders on their way to the Bull Ring, I began to get nervous, and once or twice I looked behind me thinking I was being followed.'

'But, Dad,' Mary asked, 'why didn't you come home first?'

'I was afraid if I had I would have been tempted to keep it. When I reached Great Hampton Street I knew where I was, and when I reached St George's Church I sat down on one of the benches and began to think. Oh God, Mary, how tempted I was, thinking why not keep the money and get away and make a new life for myself, or take one of the five-pound notes and get myself a shave, a haircut and a meal. But I knew wherever I tried to change it shopkeepers would look and ask where I'd got it from and maybe send for the police. Then I thought if I returned the wallet intact as I had found it, maybe he would give me some kind of reward.'

'And did he, Dad?' Mary and I asked both together.

'Well,' he began again, 'the factory I'd been looking for was opposite St George's Church in Great Russell Street where I'd been sitting. After a long wait I looked across the road and saw a brass plate with the name William Hoskins and Son, Brass Castors, on a big worn oak door. I saw the gentleman enter, waited a while, and then walked across the road and rang the bell. Soon a side door opened and an elderly workman appeared. "We ain't got no vacancies!" he yelled out. But before he could shut the door I put my foot there. "I ain't come for no job," I told him. "You tell Mr Hopkins I wish to see him, and if he wants to know who I am, tell him it's the porter and it's urgent that I see him. If you don't do what I ask you'll be sorry. Now what's it to be, or do I have to force my way in?" "All right", he replied, "yer betta follow me."

'As soon as Mr Hoskins was told, I was asked to go into the office straight away. As I entered I said, "I haven't come for a job, sir. I've come ter bring yer wallet."

'"My wallet! But how did you come by it?" he asked. When I explained how I'd carried his luggage and parcels, and how he came to drop it, he recognised me at once. "I remember you now, but I didn't know I'd lost it," he told me.

'I handed the wallet over and stood there while he checked everything was there. He thanked me and gave me one of the five-pound notes. I thanked him and touched my cap, and as I went to go out he called me back. "What did you say your name was?" he asked. "I didn't, sir. But my name is Samuel Greenhill, and as you know I work as a porter on Snow Hill station for tips. I don't like the job, sir," I told him, "but what can you do when there are no jobs to be found."

'"Well," he replied, "you'd better sit down, I may find you a part-time job."

'I couldn't believe my ears when he asked me if I knew anything about brass casting. When I replied no, he asked if I was willing to learn. Eagerly I replied, "Oh, yes, sir! Yes, sir!"

'"Trade is not very busy at the moment", he said, "but as you may have heard there's talk of war coming and that's when trades will pick up everywhere."

'He must have took a liking to me, for I'm to start work Monday at twenty shillings a week. He said it was a trial, but if he was satisfied with the results he would raise my wage.'

'It pays to be honest, Dad. I'm so happy for yer, it's about time, you deserved some luck,' laughed Mary.

'Now Mum will be pleased,' I said.

'Perhaps she will when she hears the good news, have yer told her yet?' Mary asked.

'No, I tried, but she kept on and on about this bed pan she's got ter use and about jollop they keep pouring down her.'

'Well, we both wish you good luck in your new job, don't we, Katie?'

'Yes, Dad. Perhaps Mum will now be happier when you tell her.'

'Do you know anything about this brass casting?' asked Mary.

'No, luv, my trade is brick making, but I remember when I was thirteen I used to watch men in Little Hampton Street carrying bags of sand up Taylor's entry where they did castings, and I'm willing to learn until I've mastered the job. I mean ter *keep* this job, no matter how hard or how trying it is, and with my wages yer mum won't be doing any more carding hooks and eyes and linen buttons, and I know you'll be here ter help out.'

'Yes, Dad, until I get married,' Mary replied.

'But you've another three years yet.'

'No, it's not quite two now. But while I'm here I mean ter do me best to try and put some sense into Liza,' Mary told him.

'I understand, luv. Now, I wanta hurry to the market before they close and get meself a pair of corduroy trousers and a couple of union shirts.'

When he returned we saw that he was wearing the corduroys; he was also weighed down with heavy carrier bags of fruit, vegetables, meat and also a couple of rabbits, one of which I was told to take to Grandma later. Inside another bag were the union shirts and two enamel chamber pots. As soon as I saw them I cried out, 'Them'll please her, Dad!' Dad just smiled.

The following Monday morning, Dad started his new job and I started my new school. How contented we all were now that Dad was earning. There was no more reason for Frankie, Liza and me to beg for food outside Gillotts pen factory. There was more than enough food at home to fill our bellies. It was also a pleasure to see Mum's smiling face when Dad handed over his wages.

One Saturday morning while Mary and I were upstairs making the beds, we heard Mum cry out, 'I wonder where it is. I know I 'id it down 'ere.'

Mary whispered, 'Now, Katie. Now's the time to take the tin down and see what she has ter say.'

'But Mary, I'm scared. I know she'll blame me!'

'There's no reason to be scared. I just want you to stand there and see what she says.'

We crept down the stairs to find Mum on her knees sorting the ashes over, muttering, 'It's got ter be down 'ere somewhere.'

Mary calmly pushed the tin under her nose. 'Is this what yer looking for, Mum?'

Mum snatched at the tin and glared at me. 'I suppose *she* told yer where it was!'

'No, she didn't! I came across it when I was emptying the ashes, and now you can have it back, what's left of it!'

'Where's the rest?' Mum screamed as she began to count it.

'I used some of it to pay the rent and get the bed clothes out of the pawn shop, but you're welcome to what's left.'

'Yer dad'll 'ear about this!'

'You don't dare tell Dad, and neither will I if you'll be honest and don't lie to me in the future. I'm warning you, Mum! If you ever thrash Katie agen, I *will* tell Dad. Now let's forget all about it and you can put the kettle on and make us some tea.'

I was surprised to see Mum hurry to make the pot of tea. But I was sorry to think that I would now have my old job of emptying that ash well back again. I also wondered whether my mum would find another hiding place in the future.

I never understood why my mother christened me just plain Kate; I hated the name. Hearing it continually, day in and day out, 'Kate! Do this, Kate! Kate, do that! Yes, Kate 'll do that,' was too much. I decided that if a stranger asked me my name, I would reply proudly that it was Kathleen. But when my mother heard about it she said, 'Kate's plenty good enuff fer yo! Any'ow, it meks no difference what yer call yerself. What's in a name! Yer better get up them darncers (stairs) and let's 'ave no mower of yer fancy airs an' graces or yow'll feel the back of me 'and, *Kate*!'

My sister Mary had left home several weeks ago and was happily married. Liza was pleased, but Frankie and I missed her. And although Dad was now in full-time work, Mum still said she missed Mary's wages, but I knew she was not sorry she'd left. I always knew she was jealous when Dad paid too much attention to Mary. I also knew Mary and I were his favourites. Maybe that's why Mum paid more attention to Liza and often believed her lies, which was the cause of much trouble between Mum and Dad.

My dad was on shifts, sometimes nights and sometimes days. One afternoon I came home from school and saw him sitting by the roaring fire reading *Punch*. When he saw me, he said, 'You're just the one I want, luv. I want yer to go to Bibbs paper shop and fetch me two penn'orth of twist and a clay pipe, I just broke me other one. Here's a silver threepenny bit. You can keep the change and buy yerself some sweets. Hurry before it snows agen.'

(What a lot of toffees you could buy – two ounces for a halfpenny in those days, without the fancy wrappings, just put into a newspaper cone and weighed.) 'Thank you, Dad,' I called out as I hurried to the little paper shop in Albion Street, opposite the George and Dragon where Frankie, Liza and I sang carols on Christmas Eve. As Mrs Bibbs handed me the twist, pipe and sweets, she asked what time I got home from school. When I told her four o'clock, she asked if I would like a part-time job for sixpence a week. I thought how pleased Mum would be when I gave her sixpence to buy a rabbit for our dinner. 'Oh yes, Mrs Bibbs,' I replied eagerly. 'I'd love to help you in the shop.'

'No, dear. I need someone to deliver the *Birmingham Mail* and *Dispatch* to my customers.'

'But I thought Stanley Brookes delivered them?'

'He did, dear, but his mother came in today to say that he's got German measles. Would you like to ask your mother if you could come?' she added.

I knew my mum would only say no so I made some kind of excuse for not telling her. 'How long will it take me to deliver?' I asked.

'Only about half an hour at the most, but if you hurry you could do it in much less. It's me few regulars who always have their papers delivered. I'd go myself but it's me rheumatics and I can't leave the shop.'

As soon as I had given Dad his baccy and pipe I asked if I could go out to play. 'Yes, luv, but don't go far. Yer know what yer mum is, if she finds yer not in.' After pecking Dad's cheek I ran back to the paper shop where Mrs Bibbs' face was all smiles. When I said I would be pleased to help she said, 'Here's the list. It's only just down Pope Street, numbers nine, eleven, thirteen, fifteen, seventeen and nineteen.' I was surprised that there were only six houses, and when I asked if that was all, she replied, 'Yes, dear. My other customers fetch their own.' I thought this was going to be the easiest sixpence I would ever earn, and if I pleased her she would let me be her regular paper girl.

I shall never forget that bitterly cold, wet afternoon in March, as I hurried with the bag of newspapers over my shoulder. As soon as I knocked on the door of number nine an old lady hobbling on a stick answered. She asked who I was and where the regular boy was. I told her he was ill and handed over the paper, holding out my hand for the halfpenny (which was the cost of the paper in those days).

As I waited, she said, 'My brother pays at the end of the week.'

Off I went to knock on number eleven. The door swung open and a large woman stood on the step glaring down at me. She reminded me of a pouter pigeon. 'What do yo' want, bangin' on me dower! We ain't deaf in 'ere!'

I began to get scared. 'I'm sorry, Mrs, er, er . . .'

'Ubbles the name!' she exclaimed.

'Well, Mrs Ubbles, I've brought yer *Mail*.'

'I don't 'ave the *Mail*. I 'ave the *Dispatch*.'

I handed her the paper and held out my hand for the money. She glared at me.' 'I never pay at the dower!' she yelled as she slammed it in my face.

I began to wonder if Mrs Bibbs' customers were all as bad tempered, but when I called at number thirteen there was no answer. After knocking several times I pushed the *Mail* through the letterbox, hoping it was the right one and hoping number fifteen was out too.

I was now cold and wet through, with my hair like rats' tails, wishing I was home by a cheerful fire. I banged on the door of number fifteen to be answered by a big hefty feller who stood on the top step. I noticed his grubby well-worn shirt open right down to his navel. As he hitched up his trousers I saw a thick mass of black frizzy hair, and as he snatched the paper from my hands I heard a woman's loud voice from inside. 'Shut that bleedin' dower! The draughts blowin' the smoke back down the chimney!'

The door slammed shut as he went inside, but I had to have at least one coin to show Mrs Bibbs I'd tried, so I picked up the courage to knock again. As soon as he opened the door he yelled, 'What yer want now? Bugger orf befower I put me bleedin' foot behind yer!'

I didn't wait to ask for the halfpenny, I fled down the street. I had had enough; I was hungry and miserable. I didn't bother about numbers seventeen and nineteen.

I made my way back to the shop thinking that if these were the kind of people I had to deliver to, Mrs Bibbs could find someone else. When I told her they wouldn't pay me she said, 'I'm sorry, dear, I forgot to tell you they pay at the end of the week.'

'Anyway, Mrs Bibbs,' I replied, 'I think you had better find someone else. I'm going home to a nice warm fire and to get me wet clothes off before me mum comes home.'

'I'm sorry, Kate. Here's a penny for your trouble.'

As I went to walk away after thanking her for the penny, she asked, 'Do you think your brother or sister could come?'

'I think Frankie would come but I'm certain Mum wouldn't let Liza do it. I'll ask,' I replied.

As soon as I got indoors, Mum was there to greet me with, 'An' where do yer think yo've bin till now? Yer look like a drownded rat!'

'Now, Polly,' Dad piped up. 'Wait till the wench has took her wet clothes off, then she can explain.' As Frankie threw the hessian towel for me to dry my hair, I began to explain what had happened.

'But why didn't you tell me when I sent yer for me baccy?' Dad replied.

'I thought earning sixpence a week would buy Mum a rabbit for dinner.'

Suddenly Liza butted in, 'Yo only thought that, but you'd 'ave 'ad second thoughts!'

'You shut yer trap, Liza!' Frankie exclaimed. 'We ain't all dishonest like you.'

'That's enough from you, too,' Dad shouted. 'Polly! Get the wench a drop of whisky before she gets pneumonia.'

As soon as I had drunk the warm tea and whisky I felt warmer. Then, after I'd put on dry clothes, Dad moved further away from the fire to make way for me to explain more fully what really happened. As soon as I gave him more details, he turned to Mum and asked if she knew about it.

''Er don't tell me where she goos so . . .'

'I do, Mum, but you never listen, that's why I never

tell you anything. You always listen to lies that Liza makes up about us and . . .'

'Yo just shut yer mouth befower I shut it fer yer!' Mum yelled.

'You'll do no such thing while I'm here, Polly,' Dad intervened. 'If I find yer ever lay a hand on her you'll answer to me. Now let's hear no more about it and have a bit of peace.'

After a few moments silence, Frankie asked, 'Dad, if Mrs Bibbs wants a paper boy, I could do it.'

'Yes, son, it would keep yer off the streets, but get all the details beforehand.'

Frankie sprang up off the wooden sofa, but before he could get to the door Mum said, 'You'll sit yerself down and git yer grub down yer fust!'

I never saw my brother gobble his food down so quickly. Our meal only consisted of thick slices of bread scraped with dripping and a watered down cup of tea, but each night we had our usual secret meetings outside Gillotts Pen Factory, begging for leftover food from the workers leaving the premises.

I was pleased when Mrs Bibbs gave Frankie the regular job, and after he gave Mum five pennies he often shared the other penny with me. After doing the paper round and other extras, he began to earn an extra fourpence. He never told Mum or Liza, so Mum had the usual five pennies and he shared the rest with me. Frankie kept that part-time job until he left school at fourteen when Dad got him a full-time job in a brass foundry.

Camden Grove, where we lived, was a cobbled alley with

several overcrowded back-to-back bug-infested hovels. This alley led into Camden Street and Summer Row, where omnibuses made their way into the city past more back-to-back living quarters, small dilapidated shops and several pubs. How well I remember their names: The Leopard, The Golden Cup, The King Edward and The White Horse. The last was a posh pub on the corner of Congreve Street opposite the Art Gallery and a stone's throw from the fountain where many of us kids would paddle in the clear water, until 'Bobby' (the police) came to chase us away.

At the top of the sand pits was the Nelson and a few yards further on was the Free House. I thought it was where they gave free beer, and so I wasn't surprised when many people seemed to have had too much. My school days were some of the happiest days of my young life; although many of us were ragged and often hungry, we shared what little we had. Neighbours would also help out with each other's needs. If it was possible, there was always a helping hand. Children would fetch neighbours' errands or take their younger children for walks for a few toffees or a piece of bread pudding. I loved to take the little ones in my 'go-cart' which was made from an orange box. Frankie and I would try to squeeze four children in, but if we couldn't manage it, we would take turns to carry one.

Sometimes other kids in our block would come along with us to play hide and seek, while someone would keep a look out for the wardens or the Vicar, who would chase us off with a stick. We loved hiding behind the tomb-stones. Ninety years ago we kids named the local church-yard 'Titty-bottle Park', but it was not a park, it was a place to play while the small babes in the go-cart sucked at their bottles of watered-down milk and then fell asleep. There wasn't a proper park for miles, only cobbled narrow streets and alleyways.

My mother always grumbled when she saw the go-cart. 'Bleedin' rubbish,' she would say. 'An' if I see it under me bloody feet agen I'll chop it up for firewood!' So I kept it down the cellar where I knew it would be safe. Mum was scared to go down there for coal or any rubbish to put on the fire. She would stand at the top of the steps and throw the bucket down, then she would yell into the dark at the top of her voice, 'I'm comin' down now yer bleedin' varmints.' The rats were scared of Mum, and our galvanised bucket had had so many batterings it looked more like a concertina.

I was eleven years old when I was sent home from school for scratching myself. Many schoolchildren had lice and nits in those days. Worse still was scabies or the itch, as some called it. Girls would be sent home or to the school clinic, and that day I was one of them. But I was too scared to go to the clinic; I knew from experience how rough these women could be. Instead, I ran home.

As soon as my mother saw me rubbing my back up and down the edge of the stairs door she yelled, 'Wot's the matter with yer now!?'

'It's me back, it's itching all over,' I replied.

'Well, never mind about that now, I want yer ter goo ter yer grans an' ask 'er ter lend me 'er iron. An' 'urry yerself afower I'm too late fer the pawn shop!'

As I hurried out to my grandma's, my back was feeling sore where I had rubbed it, and when grandma saw me fidgeting she asked me what was wrong. When I told her she said, 'Why couldn't yer mum 'ave looked at it before sendin' yer 'ere in the cold?'

'She was in a hurry, Grandma, for the loan of yer iron.'

'Never mind the bloody iron! Just lift yer frock up an' drop yer drawers down. Let's look at yer.'

As soon as she took one look at me she cried, 'Oh my God, you've got chicken pox! Yer better stay 'ere while I goo and fetch the doctor.'

The doctor told my grandma I had German measles, and then said, 'Give her plenty of saffron tea to drink and one of these pills three times a day. Keep her bowels well open and don't let her face any strong light. I'll call again in two days' time.'

When I heard I was to stay with my gran I was delighted, but I worried that my mum would be waiting for the iron. Gran cried out, 'Never mind the bloody iron! Get yer clothes back on and I'll deal with 'er when she comes.'

As I began to get dressed, in walked my mother. I knew there was going to be an argument when she yelled out, 'Wot's 'er doin' 'ere, Hannah, 'alf undressed when I sent 'er ter borra' yer iron?'

'Did yer know this child was ill?' Grandma asked.

'She was all right when I sent 'er 'ere ter borra yer iron.'

'Never mind the bloody iron, if yo'd bothered ter look at 'er yo'd 'ave sin the rash!'

'Wot yer talkin' about?' Mum asked.

'Er's got German measles.'

'Who said so?'

'Doctor Robinson. I fetched 'im in!' Grandma told her.

'Well, as soon as she gets 'er frock on I'll tek 'er back 'ome right now!' Mum exclaimed.

'Yo'll do no such thing,' Grandma yelled back, 'she's stayin' 'ere. Yer know what'll 'appen if yer tek 'er out in this freezin' weather. So the best thing yer can do is 'elp me push me bed up ter the wall. She's ter sleep with me until she gets betta.'

'I ain't got time! I got me ironin' ter do ready for the pawn shop!'

'Well, yer can ask one of yer neighbours ter lend yer theirs. Yo ain't 'avin' mine an' that's that!' Grandma added.

'Thanks fer nothin'!' Mum yelled as she bounced out.

Grandma yelled back, 'Yer a bloody selfish 'ard-'earted cow!'

But Mum just shrugged her shoulders and left.

As soon as she'd gone, Grandma told me to sit by the fire in the kitchen while she went to ask her neighbour to help move her bed by the wall.

'I wun't be long,' she called out, 'but I don't want ter tell 'er yer've got measles. I'll just say yer stayin' with me fer a bit.'

I don't know what she actually told her but Mrs Turner came with no questions asked. As soon as they came downstairs I saw Grandma give her a drop of gin in a cup, and after thanking her, she left.

'Now tek all yer clothes off an' put this calico shift on,

then I want yer ter tek this pill and drink yer saffron tea, then I'll tek yer up ter me warm bed.' The shift was like a bell tent which almost smothered me, and when Gran saw me pull a face at the tea she cried out, 'Now come, let's see yer drink it all down! I know it tastes bitter, but if yer don't drink it yo'll get worse, an' yer know wot that'll mean. Yer mum'll 'ave yer sent to the infirmary.'

Often Grandma's words of wisdom were spoken sharply, but she always meant well and I loved her for her kindness to others who also needed help. The house where she lived alone was in Icknield Street, ten minutes' walk from our house. She only had one living room, a kitchen, a small bedroom and a box room. There was not much furniture, and what she had was old and well worn but clean.

She told me to go upstairs while she locked up. Upstairs I noticed there was the three-quarter iron bedstead with straw mattress, striped flocked bedding, a bolster, a pillow, two blue flannelette sheets and a blanket of many colours which I hadn't seen before when I had mumps. In the little iron gate a small fire was burning, and on the hearth was a threadbare piece of carpet. Beneath the window was a dressing table with a water jug and crock basin. Although everything was worn and faded, it was still warm and cheerful. How different from that cold, dismal attic where I usually slept with my brother and sister, fighting over the coats that covered us. There was no smell of the lime-washed walls at Grandma's; she had pretty wallpaper with red roses.

As I sat on the stool warming my toes by the fire,

Grandma entered with a hot oven plate covered with a piece of blanket, and as she pushed it down between the bed covers she told me to get into bed. She put the little fire out and got in beside me, putting her arms around me. Although I was happy to be with her, I began to worry – what if Grandma caught my measles, who would look after us both? When I asked her she replied, 'Don't worry, I've 'ad all the diseases allotted ter me in my lifetime, whoopin' cough, mumps, chicken pox, even diphtheria, an' I'm still 'ere!'

'Grandma,' I said, 'I'd love to live with you for ever.'

'That's impossible, luv, but yer can always come an' see me when yer school 'olidays begin.'

My dad came each night after work, before he went home, and he always brought me an orange or a bottle of ginger pop. Every time he said good night to me and Grandma I felt sad; I loved my dad, he was kind and thoughtful. If only my mum had had half the same feelings for us, life would have been better for all concerned.

My mother never came once during my illness, but as soon as dad told her I was much better she came to say that the school inspector had called and I had to be in school the following Monday morning, or dad would be summonsed.

When Grandma asked the doctor if I was fit to go to school, he told her I was very thin owing to the illness, but that if she would go down to the dispensary the nurse would give her a bottle of Parish's Food and some tablets. I was also to attend him once a week. I don't know what the tablets were but after a couple of days I was feeling well again. I was also sad knowing that I had to go home; I knew I would miss those nights when my grandma used to read to me from a magazine, or stories from the *War Cry* and *Little Soldier* which she brought home from the Salvation Army Mission she often attended. One day I saw her writing a letter to someone, and being curious to know why my mum couldn't read or write, I asked Grandma for the reason.

'Dain't she ever tell yer why?' she asked.

'No, Grandma, and I'm too scared to ask, but I did overhear my dad say Mum was illiterate, and there are often tempers flyin' when he offers to teach her. I'm glad Dad helped me to read and write, I'm now top of the class thanks to him. Which school did you go to, Grandma?' I added.

'I never went to no school, luv, I was sent inter service when I was not much older than you. Me mum an' dad were always doin' moonlight flits, an' when I was five we went ter live in the Black Country, just outside West Bromwich. Lots of little girls like me dain't goo ter school, they stayed ter 'elp in the 'ome where there was big families, an' I 'elped me mum ter chop and sell firewood ter the villagers. I made friends with one little girl who taught me ter read an' write in 'er fashion, an' when I began ter talk an' write in 'er dialect, me mum an' dad often laughed at me!'

I knew Grandma never could pronounce her words properly, but I understood her. When I offered to teach her she said she was too long in the tooth.

'But my dad speaks properly,' I said.

'Yes, luv, yer grandad saw that 'e was sent to a good public school fer boys only.'

I was very inquisitive to learn more about my parents and grandparents, and when I asked her to explain them to me, she replied, 'Well, Katie, yer nearly twelve now, so I think it's time I told yer something mower. When is yer next school 'oliday?' she asked.

'Easter, Grandma,' I replied.

'Very well, yo cum an' see me, but not on Good Friday, that's me day I goo ter the Mission.'

When I asked Mum if I could go to Grandma's I don't think she heard me. It was a bitterly cold morning that holiday Monday, and I ran all the way to her house to keep warm. As soon as I walked in I saw her sitting in her rocking chair beside a roaring fire, and I went up to her and kissed her on the cheek. She cried out, 'I dain't 'ear yow cum in, I must be gettin' deaf in me old days! Any'ow, get yer tammy and coat off and draw up a chair ter the fire while I goo an' fill the kettle.'

'You stay in the warm Grandma, I'll do it,' I told her.

'Thank you, luv,' she replied.

When I went down the yard I saw one of Grandma's neighbours trying to fill a large enamel jug. As the tap began to dribble she asked if I'd come to stay again.

'Only for today,' I replied.

''Ow is she an' 'ow's 'er legs?' she asked.

'I don't know, she never complains, Mrs Turner,' I told her as I turned and hurried indoors.

When I got back in Grandma seemed to be asleep. I put the kettle on and when it began to boil I heard her say, 'Is that the kettle I can 'ear singin'?'

'Yes, Grandma, I'm just going to make a nice cup of tea.'

'While yer mekin' the tea I'll do us some toast and drippin', I've saved yer some of the brown drippin' 'an jelly at the bottom of the basin, wot yer like.'

But I wasn't really hungry for bread and dripping; I was only hungry for the stories she had promised to tell me. After we had finished eating our toast and had another cup of tea, she said, 'Now Katie, luv, pull up yer chair ter the fire, then I'll tell yer about me past befower it's too late, but yer must remember ter keep it ter yerself. An' yer must promise me yer wunt breathe a word ter yer mum or dad, or anybody else, until it's necessary.'

'Yes, Grandma, I promise on my honour,' I replied as she began to relate her past.

'When I was thirteen an' my sister Nancy was fifteen, we did a moonlight flit agen. It was the last slums we ever lived in, much worse than they are terday. There was only one small livin' room, an' one bedroom, an' a cubby 'ole across the narra landin' where me an Nancy slept. We 'ad rats but we got used ter them, any'ow they was more frightened of us than we o' them, but when we lit our candle we killed mower cockroaches in one night than we 'ad 'ot dinners in a twelve-month. There wus no back yard or even a dry closet, so if we was cut short we 'ad ter goo an' find a patch down the lane an' cover it over with a shovel.'

'Oh Grandma, how awful, couldn't you find somewhere better to live?' I asked.

'The neighbours all around this sleepy little village were in the same boat as us, luv, there was no better place fer miles, just fields where everybody struggled ter earn a livin'. Mum's rent was then two shillin' a week, an' sometimes she found it 'ard ter pay that, when Dad spent money on drink.

'Me dad was very 'andsome an' so was me mum, but she wasn't the pretty woman any more after 'e'd come 'ome the werst fer drink an' knock 'er about. She was never without a black eye, an' once 'e broke 'er nose when she told 'im 'ed bin sleepin' with another woman.'

'But why couldn't you get the police to stop him, Grandma?' I asked.

'Nancy did, an' 'e calmed down, but after a few days 'e was worse. Nancy and me often seen 'im arm in arm gooin' across the fields with other young women, but we was too scared ter tell Mum. If 'e knew we'd bin spyin' on 'im 'e would 'ave leathered us with 'is belt, an' we couldn't run away, nor 'ide from 'im, only ter the neighbours, an' they 'ad their own troubles. Any'ow 'e'd 'ave found us wherever we went.

'Now, Katie,' she went on, 'I don't know 'ow much yer know about the wiles of men, but yer should know more about life and their wicked plausible ways before yer grow older, an' if yer mum ain't already told yer, then I'm gooin' ter tell yer now. But yer mustn't ferget yer promise.'

'But me dad ain't wicked, he's kind and good,' I replied.

'God ferbid! I dain't say all men, luv, me an' yer grandad brought our Sam an' 'is brothers up ter be respected an' 'onest. Now don't interrupt. I'll tell yer about yer mum an' dad later, an' the things yo should know about life.'

'I'm sorry, Grandma, I'll try not to,' I said.

'Any'ow, luv, I think we'll 'ave another cuppa, me throat's as dry as a bone, I 'aven't talked so much fer years. Ye'll find the gin bottle in the cupboard,' she added.

I was now so eager to know more that I couldn't make that pot of tea quick enough. After pouring the gin in a cup, she drank it down and gave a big sigh.

'That feels betta, luv, now where was I?' she asked.

'You said my dad was respected.'

'Oh yes,' she said, as she sat back in her rocking chair. 'Yer dad was 'andsome too, still is, an' 'e used ter sing in the choir when 'e was a young lad, but I'll tell yer about that later. Now wot I'm goin' ter try an' tell yer now, I know might shock yer, but it's sommat yo oughta know, an' ter warn yer as I've said about the lies and plausible wiles of men ter pretty gels like yo,' she told me. I was all ears.

'Two days a wick our mum went out cleanin' fer the farmer's wife, when she'd bring 'ome leftover food, but we were all glad ter eat it wotever it was. Some nights Mum come 'ome very late an' would find me father in drink in bed. One night Mum was workin' late at the farm'ouse, an' while we was in bed I 'eard me father's drunken steps cummin' up the stairs an' 'e called out fer me momma. I pretended to be asleep but when he came in our room I saw 'im goo over ter where Nancy slept. I 'eard him whisper, "Are yer awake, Nancy luv?" She dain't answer. I didn't know then but she pretended ter be asleep. When 'e started ter stroke 'er face I whispered, 'She's asleep.'

'"Oh well, you'll do," I 'eard 'im say. I dain't know

wot 'e meant until 'e lay on top o' me an' lifted up me chimmy. I tried ter push 'im off me, an' when I began ter scream Nancy came ter me rescue. '"No! No! Not 'er!' I 'eard 'er yell. Just then Mum came in the room. When she saw wot 'e'd tried ter do she kicked an' punched 'im, then Nancy and me began ter join in and we finished up by kickin' 'im down the stairs. 'E was too drunk ter retaliate, 'e almost ran out o' the 'ouse, and after Mum bolted the door she cried out, "Yo'll both sleep with me in future."

'We never saw 'im agen. Three days later the police came ter tell Mum they had found 'im lyin' naked at the side of the canal with 'is throat cut. Nobody found out who murdered 'im, but Mum said it must 'ave bin one of 'is whores or one of their 'usbands.'

Just as she was about to relate some more, we heard a knock on the door.

'Come in,' Grandma called out, but when we saw it was Liza she cried out, 'An' wot der yer want?'

'Mum's sent me ter fetch Katie.'

'Well, yer can goo back an' tell yer mum I'll send 'er back when I'm ready! No need ter sen yo!' she added.

'Yer don't like me, Granny, but I don't like you either!' Liza replied as she stuck her tongue out.

'As long as yer know!' Grandma called out, 'Now bugger off afower I clout yer bloody ear'ole, yer cheeky young bugger!'

'I think I'd better go, Grandma, you know what me Mum's like if she's disobeyed.'

'Well, yer betta come in the kitchen with me first, I wanta give yer something.'

As soon as I entered, she whispered, 'Don't ferget yer promise, luv, not a word, an' come agen when yer can, if yer want ter 'ear some more.'

'Yes, Grandma, I'll try tomorrow,' I whispered, 'and I won't forget.'

'An' 'ere's some 'umbugs,' she called out, 'ter share amongst yer.'

I thanked her and kissed her on the cheek, then followed Liza out into the street. We hadn't gone but a couple of paces when Liza asked, 'What's that yer ain't got ter forget?'

'To call agen,' I replied.

'But why was yer whisperin' in the kitchen?' she asked.

'You got yer ear to the keyhole agen?' I said.

'No I never, an' yer can keep yer humbugs!'

'Please yourself,' I replied as she ran off.

When I arrived indoors I saw Dad looking over his glasses and reading *Punch* as he sat by the fire.

As soon as Mum saw me she said, 'Yo took yer time ter get 'ere!'

'I came as soon as Liza told me, Mum,' I replied.

'But that was nearly an 'our agoo, it don't tek ten minutes from yer gran's. Where yer bin till now, an' I want the truth!'

Suddenly Dad threw his paper across the room and stared at Mum over the top of his glasses as he cried out, 'Polly, for goodness sake! Leave the wench alone, carn't yer see she's telling yer the truth? Wait till Liza gets back and hear what she has to say.'

As soon as Liza came in Mum didn't have time to ask. Dad sprang off his chair and as he went towards her he asked, 'And where have you been till now?'

'I went ter fetch Katie from Gran's,' was her reply.

'Well, it didn't take you nearly an hour, now I want ter know where you've been and the truth!' Dad told her.

'I went ter see me friend first, before I went ter me gran's,' Liza answered.

Dad pushed her away from him and cried out, 'There's yer answer, Polly, now let me read with a bit of peace.'

The next morning was the last day of the holiday before I had to start back to school, so I asked my mum if I could go to Grandma's again. 'I want some jobs doin' 'ere first, then I'll think about it.'

After I ate my porridge, I went down to the tap in the yard, and when I'd finished filling the brewhouse boiler I had to fetch slack up from the cellar, and after chopping up some sticks of wood to go under the furnace she said I could go, but be back before six o'clock.

I knew I could still spend several hours with my grandma. I put on my woollen hat and shabby brown coat and hurried out before she could change her mind. But just then Dad appeared and stopped me. 'Where's Katie off to in such a hurry?' he asked Mum.

'She's gooin' ter yer mother's agen,' Mum told him.

'I'm surprised yer lettin' her go after yesterday.'

'She's done 'er jobs. Any'ow, it's one less mouth ter feed.'

'Very well,' Dad said, 'off yer go, but yer brother will fetch yer back this time.'

'Six o'clock, remember!' I heard Mum call out.

As soon as I got to Grandma's I noticed the kettle was

already on and the table laid with two saucers, cups and four dishes. When I asked if she was expecting visitors, she replied, 'Yes, luv, I knowed yerd come. I've boiled some bacon bones an' split peas, an' there's treacle an' bread puddin' I've med fer afters.'

'My dad says you spoil me, Grandma,' I told her.

'P'raps I do, but yer a wench after me own 'eart, an' I'll always luv yer whatever 'appens. Are yer ready fer yer dinner?' she asked.

'Yes, Grandma, I only had me porridge this morning.'

'Well, sit yerself up ter the table while I dish the soup out, then we'll 'ave our bread puddin' an' treacle. After that we'll pull our chairs up by the fire and I'll tell yer the rest of me story afower it's too late.'

I often wondered why she kept saying, 'before it's too late'. Was she going somewhere without telling me? Maybe she would tell me later, I thought. When we had finished our meal and that delicious bread pudding and black treacle, I helped to wash the dishes, and after placing them in the cupboard we drew our chairs up to the fire. Just then Grandma said she had to go upstairs and fetch her clean underwear to be aired on the clothes horse.

'I'll fetch 'em, Grandma,' I told her, 'you rest yer legs.'

'Thank yer, luv, they 'ave bin playin' me up terday.'

When I came back downstairs I watched her place them on the clothes horse beside the fireplace. When she turned round I noticed she looked very pale. I was worried. 'Are you all right, Grandma? You look tired. Would you like to go up and rest and I'll bring yer a nice cuppa tea with plenty of gin, then yer can finish about yer life another day?' I asked her.

'I'll be all right, luv, it's just me legs, an' I must try an' finish tellin' yer before it's too late.'

There were those words again.

'Anyway, where did I leave off when Liza came?' she asked.

'It was about the police coming ter tell you about the murder, Grandma.'

'Oh yes, I remember. They never did find out who done it, but I think some of the villagers knew, but we didn't care. We was all well rid of 'im, and I think the people in the village too.

'After 'e was buried we were all much 'appier for a while. Then one night while Mum was out, I 'eard Nancy cryin' in the bedroom, an' I went in ter see why. She tried ter tell me she was goin' away. When I asked 'er where and why, she said, "Hannah, I can't tell." I asked if Mum was sendin' 'er ter be in service but she said, "No, it's worse than that!" Then suddenly she flung 'er arms 'round me sobbin', "I'm goonta 'ave a babby, Hannah," she said. I couldn't believe me ears when she told me it was me father's. I asked 'er if she'd told Mum, but she said she had been too scared as Father 'ad promised ter cut 'er throat an' throw 'er in the canal if she told anyone.

"But you'll 'ave ter tell Mum," I said, "she'll find out."

"I'm goin' ter tell 'er I'm gooin away ter werk on a farm," she said.

"But where are yer really gooin', Nancy, please tell me." I pleaded with 'er ter tek me with 'er, but she said when she'd found another place ter live she'd come back fer me. That night we flung our arms around each other and wept.

'A few days later, neither Mum nor me could understand Nancy's moods, and when she went off 'er food Mum took 'er ter the doctor. When 'e told 'er me sister was 'avin a babby, Mum almost dragged 'er thro' the village, and as soon as she come indoors Mum began ter beat 'er with a stick. When I tried ter tek it off 'er she 'it me with it an' yelled that I was as bad as 'er. Mum didn't stop, she wanted the truth an' Nancy lied, she said it was a chap in the village. Then Mum said he would 'ave ter marry 'er or she'd be put in an 'ome for wanton wenches.

'As soon as we 'eard 'er bedroom door slam, we lay down on our flock bed 'an cried ourselves ter sleep.' I saw Grandma's eyes fill with tears and I felt very weepy too. I also had the sad feeling I didn't want to hear any more, but being an inquisitive child I had to know more.

'Sometime durin' that night,' Grandma continued, 'Nancy must 'ave crept out of bed. She'd run away without tellin' me or Mum where she was gooin'. We made enquiries at every door in that village, and sometimes she dain't trust me ter be alone so she made me sleep with 'er. Often I would see 'er kneelin' on the floor weepin' or prayin' fer God ter bring Nancy back as she still loved 'er an' would fergive 'er. I too loved me sister and I prayed every night at the side of the bed with Mum, but our prayers were never answered. Some nights Mum would wake me up an' call me Nancy. Another night she got out of bed ter tuck me in an' I 'eard 'er say ter me, "Nancy, luv, don't listen ter Hannah's lies, she's a bad, bad wench!" Sometimes I'd

wake up ter find Mum wanderin' around outside, and I
becum frightened when she was found naked on the
canal bank w'ere me father 'ad bin murdered.

'Later, Mum was put in 'an asylum, where she died. I
was alone and nearly fourteen when I was put in an
orphan 'ome, and when I was sixteen I 'ad ter goo inter
service to a big 'ouse in Sutton Coldfield.

'I'm feelin' a bit tired now, luv, but I'll tell yer some
mower when yer cum agen. Any'ow, it's best yer get 'ome
befower it's dark, an' don't ferget! Not a word ter anybody wot I bin talkin' ter yer about.'

'Believe me, Grandma, I won't. Is there anything I
can do for yer before I go?' I asked.

'Yes, luv, will yer tek me oven plate out an' wrap it in
its bit of blanket, an' put it in me bed, then yer can rub
me swollen legs befower yer brother comes ter fetch yer.'

As I put the hot plate down the bed, I noticed how
faded and worn the bed cover was. I knew she often
wore this around her shoulders when she sat by the fire.
It was then that I thought I would save up all my farthings and halfpennies, and when I'd enough I'd buy
some pink skeins of wool to knit or crochet my grandma
a shawl.

After making her another cup of tea with gin, I rubbed
her legs with warm embrocation and then it was time for
me to go. As I kissed her cheek I heard her whisper,
'God bless yer an' don't ferget ter come agen.' My dad
also called on Grandma once a week to see how she was
faring and to bring her a small bottle of gin, unbeknown
to my mum; this was another of my secrets.

When I was halfway home, I saw my brother Frankie

coming towards me. I loved my brother for his wonderful sense of humour, but when he told me stories it was hard to know whether to believe him or not. As he reached me he began to sniff the air.

'What's that awful pong I can smell?'

'It's embrocation I use on Grandma's legs, but I don't think they're getting any better,' I replied.

'Has she seen the doctor?' he asked.

'Yes, but he says there's nothing more he can give her, only something for the pain and the liniment. Grandma says it's the cold damp weather, but Mum blames it on old age,' I told him.

'Yer don't expect any pity from Mum, do yer?' Frankie replied.

'No, I know that, but she never bothers ter go and see her, or ask me how she is.'

'Well, they always quarrel,' Frankie said.

'What about?' I asked.

'I don't know, but knowin' our mum she's selfish an' finds fault with everybody. It's no wonder the neighbours don't like 'er. Anyhow, next time yer go ter me granny's tell her it wants a pair of men's strong fingers ter massage 'er all over. I'll do me best ter cure her,' Frankie said, grinning all over his face.

'You ain't a man yet, Frankie, and anyway, she wouldn't even let yer look at them, nor me dad when he offered,' I told him.

'Why not? I've seen Dad rub Mum's legs, an' there's nothin' wrong with hers, an' I've rubbed Nellie's legs many a time, but she never lets me get past her knees,' he grinned.

'Yer never do!' I exclaimed. 'You should be ashamed, the pair of yer!'

'Why? We're gettin' married ain't we!'

'Maybe you are, but not until she's twenty-one and you've got a lot more years ter wait. She might change her mind by then,' I told him.

'Not my Nellie,' he replied, winking.

After the Easter holiday, all the girls in my class had to write an essay about the kind of things we did during the holiday. When I tried to tell my mum what I had written, she wasn't interested. When my dad came home from work I told him I had top marks for my story and he asked me what I had written. I had said how my dear old grandma was suffering from rheumatics and how I spent most of my holiday helping her. I would have loved to have written about some of the stories my grandma had told me, but she had said that until it was necessary I was to keep her secret.

Now my kind old grandma is no longer with us I believe it is time, in this day and age, for people young and old to hear the rest of Grandma's story as she told it to me the following Whitsun holiday.

'Now where was I?' she asked.

'You went into service in a big house in Sutton Coldfield,' I told her.

'Oh yes, I remember now, there was the mistress an' the master, we dain't see much o' them, the cook whose chest stood out like a pouter pigeon, an' who 'ad black beady eyes in the back of 'er 'ead. Daisy Fellers, she was the kitchen maid, and I was the scullery maid doin' all the dirty rough and smelly jobs.'

'Did you have to empty the slop bucket, Grandma, like I do for Mum?' I asked.

'Not only them, luv, but there was the night commodes too. I 'ad a shillin' an' tuppence a wick, an' Daisy 'ad fourpence more. She was a pretty wench, just seventeen. When I'd bin there a couple of wicks, we becum friends. We both 'ad one 'alf day on Mondays, an' we spent this tergether, strolling round the park an' feedin' the swans. Daisy 'ad lovely blonde 'air an' big blue eyes, she was very pretty an' very vain, always givin' young chaps the glad eye.' Grandma began to smile as she added, 'When she passed a shop winda with a mirra, she'd goo back an' preen 'erself, an 'abit I got into too. I can remember the time when I 'ad lovely long black 'air, but when I was put in the orphanage I was nearly scalped an' deloused, an' me rags was snatched off me an' burnt. I felt ashamed ter walk about, everybody seemed ter mek fun of me.'

'But why, Grandma? There's plenty of boys and girls in our school who get sent to the clinic to be deloused and scalped. I remember when I first started school, I'd only been there three weeks when the nurse came to inspect us and gave me a note. Mum nearly went mad when I showed it to her in front of all the neighbours and, after she had belted me, my dad poured vinegar over my head and almost scalped me! Mum never let me forget the shame she said I'd brought on her. But the worst of it was, Mum knitted me a skull cap to wear in school and some of the kids used to call me "Knitty Nora".'

'Yer mum fergets what it's like to be a young wench an' I 'ad ter more than delouse 'er, but that's another story, I'll tell yer later.

'When I left the orphanage and went inter service with all my written details, who I was an' where I'd come from, the mistress showed the letter ter cook an' she never let me ferget it!

'When Daisy an' me spent our 'alf days tergether, we 'ad ter be back indoor by four-thirty or we was punished, we worn't even allowed ter explain. If we tried we were sent ter bed without anything to eat, an' if we cried we were beaten with a bamboo cane. We worked 'ard an' was always 'ungry. Some nights when cook was dozin' in 'er armchair, sodden in gin, Daisy would 'elp 'erself to titbits to share with me, but I was too scared ter eat them in case cook found out. I used ter 'ide them precious pieces until I went ter me bed.'

'But, Grandma, why didn't yer tell the cook you were always hungry?' I asked.

'It wouldn't 'ave med an eyeful of difference, we was only allotted so much an' that was that! An' if Daisy 'ad 'ave bin caught she would 'ave bin dismissed, but it seemed ter me that Daisy wouldn't 'ave cared one way or the other. But it did surprise me 'ow it did really 'appen.'

I noticed then that Grandma had stopped talking and was gazing into the fire. I asked, 'Is that all, Grandma?'

'No, luv, I was thinkin' it was time we 'ad another cuppa tea an' another piece of cake. Talkin' about them titbits 'as med me feel 'ungry. Are you 'ungry, luv?' she added.

'No, Grandma, I'm interested to hear what happened to Daisy, but I'll make you a pot of tea an' cut you some cake,' I replied.

'Very well, luv, then I think I'll tell yer wot 'appened termorra.'

Maybe I was a little selfish to keep asking questions; I didn't realise how tired she was until I saw her eyes drooping, and when I asked, she replied, 'Just a bit, luv, but when I begin ter talk I never know when ter stop. Me mum used ter say I could talk the leg off an iron pot!'

When Grandma placed the embrocation bottle on the hob to warm I knew it was time for me to put the hot oven plate between the bed covers. After making the bed I hurried downstairs to make her comfortable. As I began to massage her legs I said, 'Grandma, I'd love to live here with you.'

'I'd luv ter 'ave yer, Katie, but I know yer mum would never let yer stay.'

'Well, perhaps she'll let me stay the night if I hurry home and ask her.'

'Yer can try, but if yo ain't back in an 'alf 'our I'll get up ter me bed,' Grandma said.

I kissed her wrinkled cheek and ran all the way home.

When I got indoors there was only my brother Frankie. 'Where's Mum?' I asked.

'I don't know, an' why are you out of breath?' he replied.

When I tried to explain he said, 'Mum won't let yer, *yer* know that.'

'But my grandma needs me. If I go back now will you explain to Mum?'

'No!' he replied. 'She won't listen ter me, you know that, but you can try, I think I hear 'er coming.'

But instead of my mum, I was pleased to see my dad walk in. As soon as I explained to him, he said, 'Very well, love, if yer gran needs you, you'd better leave me ter explain ter yer mum. Now off yer go before she gets home.'

'Thank yer, Dad,' I cried as I hugged and kissed him.

I don't know what my dad told my mum, but I stayed with Grandma the whole week of my Whitsun holiday. She taught me to cook and make a hot-pot, and even showed me how to make bread and cakes. While she was explaining the ingredients she began to stammer, which made me smile. I hoped she hadn't noticed, but during the afternoon when we were sat by the fire, she asked, 'Why did yer smile, luv?'

'I'm sorry, Grandma, I wasn't smiling at you, I was thinking I must have sounded worse than that when I first learned to talk. When I was about eight years old I found an old dictionary in the loft, it must have been there I don't know how many years and it had several pages torn out. I showed it to Dad and he said it would help me with my education, but Mum and Liza used to scoff at me when I read it aloud, and Mum said she'd put it on the fire if she saw me with it again.

'Sometimes I would shut myself in our communal closet, where I would try to teach myself to pronounce the words properly and what they meant, until someone would bang on the door and yell, "Are yer stayin' in there all night?"'

'I might 'ave bin a different woman if I'd bin able ter

write an' read properly,' she said. 'When we've cleared all the crocks away, I'll tell yer mower about Daisy an' 'ow I come ter meet yer grandpa.'

'But I don't want yer to get too tired and talk the leg off an iron pot,' I replied, and she started to laugh. I always remember that you could laugh with her but never at her.

As we sat facing each other by the fire, she began to tell me about Daisy, and how she came to meet Grandpa Edward. I often saw that faraway look in her eyes when she was trying to explain. Grandma began, 'I often saw Daisy talkin' ter a young man in the park. Once I asked 'er who 'e was an' she told me she'd known 'im a long time an' that one day they was gooin' ter elope. She'd said it too many times, Katie, and I dain't believe 'er, until one afternoon I asked cook where she was. All that cook said was that she'd run away an' I was ter get on with me jobs. I was too nervous ter ask any more questions, but each time I went ter the park I 'oped an' prayed she'd be there. Then one afternoon, feeling weepy an' lonely, I sat meself down on a bench an' a young man I'd never seen afower came and sat down beside me. Straight away 'e asked me if I was waitin' for someone, and when I told 'im about Daisy 'e said 'e 'adn't seen 'er, but 'ad often seen us together.

''E asked me me name, an' when I told 'im 'e said 'e'd 'ad a sister called Hannah, but she died with the fever.'

'What fever was that, Grandma?' I asked.

'Scarlet fever,' she replied, 'now don't interrupt, luv, I must get on,' she told me smiling. ''E then told me 'is mum's name was Martha, an' 'is name was Edward, but 'e said 'e'd like me ter call 'im Ted.'

'But, Grandma, wasn't you scared being alone with a strange man?'

'No, luv, there was other people passin' us, an' any'ow I was glad of 'is company an' wanted somebody ter talk to. 'E was so 'ansome an' polite, Katie, I dain't feel a bit shy.

'On me next afternoon off we sat by the bandstand listenin' ter the band, 'an when 'e took 'old of me 'and and said I was the prettiest girl 'ed ever seen, no one 'ad ever said that ter me afower, an' I was flattered an' 'ad the funniest feelin' I thought was luv. Like an innocent child that I was.'

'Did you tell him you loved him?' I asked.

'No, girls never told a man in those days, not until 'e said 'e luved *you*.'

'But did he say he loved you, Grandma?'

'No, Katie, 'e never did, I 'ad ter find out later whether 'e did or not ter me sorrow. That's what I'm tryin' ter explain, there are different kinds of luv,' she replied. 'There's the feelin' yer 'ave fer yer mum an' dad, an' brothers an' sisters or friends, even a cat or dog or a toy, but wot I'm tryin' ter say is it's a different kind of luv between a man an' a woman. It could be true luv an' bein' adored, or it could be a foolish feelin' between two people, but I wanta explain that later.'

I was expecting Grandma to say, 'Before it's too late', but she said, as she began to smile, 'Before I talk the leg off the iron pot.' Grandma seldom smiled, but when she did she looked so comical with only her two front teeth which she called her pickled onion fork; but I loved my dear old grandma for all that.

I tried to understand all that she tried to explain, when she said, 'One day 'e asked me if I'd meet 'is mum. I was thrilled, an' when 'e said 'e wanted ter marry me, I gave me notice in an' left after grumbles an' warnin's from cook an' the mistress. But I ignored their warnin's, I was too 'appy ter care.

'I never expected such a warm welcome 'is dear old ma gave me. When she threw 'er arms round me, I knew at once I was goin' ter like 'er. "Come in, my dear, an' sit yerself by the fire while I put the kettle on the fire an' mek yer a cup of tea" I 'eard 'er say just as Ted put 'is overcoat coat on an' said 'e was wanted at the Mission. I felt disappointed when 'e went out the 'ouse without another word ter me or 'is ma.'

'But, Grandma, didn't he kiss yer or say ta-ta?'

'I never thought about it, Katie, I was too interested in lookin' around and tekin' in all the surroundin's. There was this nice livin' room, an' another room facin' which she called 'er parlour, then she showed me the kitchen, a scullery with 'ot an' cold water, an' at the back of the 'ouse was a pretty little flower garden. Then she showed me the three bedrooms, includin' the one I 'ad ter sleep in. Everywhere was clean an' furnished, although old an' worn, but this was a palace ter what I'd bin used to. But then I was an orphan, a nobody, so who was I ter pick an' choose when this 'andsome man asked me ter marry 'im.

'Martha said I was ter call 'er Ma and that 'er son was twenty-one and was a builder. 'E was also in the

Salvation Army band and choir. Then Ma said 'is father
'ad been drowned at sea an' 'e was an only son. When
she asked about my family I told 'er about Mum an' me
sister an' that I was seventeen. I was careful not ter tell
'er about me father, I just said 'e died suddenly an' 'ow I
came ter be in an orphan 'ome, an' in service. I could see
she was beginnin' ter like me. "Well, dear, there's a home
for yer here an' I hope you'll be 'appy." Then she asked
me if 'er son 'ad asked me ter marry 'im.

'When I said yes, she replied, "Well, dear, I wish ter
give you a bit of advice. My son gets very temperamen-
tal at times, but if you can put up with 'is moods, you'll
find you'll be 'appy, but be patient, dear". She also said
'er would always be there if I needed 'er. I loved that
dear old lady, she was the only real friend I ever 'ad, she
was lovable, kind and understanding.

A few weeks later when I became pregnant I dain't
know then that I was gooin' ter 'ave a babby. I put me
weight down ter the good meals I was eatin', but when
Ma told me I was about three months pregnant, I was
surprised but 'appy. She asked if I'd told 'er son, but I
said we were not on speakin' terms, but it was best I
should tell 'im. When I told 'im he dain't seem very
pleased, an' after 'e put up the banns 'e was grumpy and
disagreeable, but I ignored 'is moods. I remember the
laugh Ma an' me 'ad when 'er tried ter pull in me corsets
tighter, an' the old-fashioned smock I'd 'ave ter wear so
that nosy people couldn't see that I wasn't a virgin, but I
was 'appy ter be wed. Durin' me pregnancy, me 'usband
began ter get very grumpy an' sit fer 'ours without a
word. Ma said men suffered in different ways when a

woman was pregnant, so I put it down ter that. Five months later when I began ter 'ave terrible sharp pains, it was then that Ma told me she'd bin a midwife, an' I was not ready. A month later I gave birth to an 'ealthy baby, 'e was luvley. I was so 'appy an' so was Ma, it was 'er first grandson, but I noticed me 'usband seldom looked at 'im, an' when I told 'im wot I was gooin' ter name the babby, that was our first big quarrel.

'I wanted our son ter be named Samuel, but when 'is father said 'e wanted 'im named after 'im, I was adamant. I told 'im *I* was the one that 'ad given birth an' *I* was gooin' ter name 'im Samuel. Well, 'e lost 'is temper and smacked me face twice an' I never forgave 'im. Although 'e still gav me the 'ousekeepin' money, I knew 'e was mean, and where he spent 'is late nights I never asked agen. I wouldn't believe 'im or 'is excuses.

'When yer daddy began ter walk an' talk, I noticed 'e was pickin' up the words like me. I knew I couldn't explain ter 'im any betta, but I was glad when Ted took over an' when 'e was five years old 'e paid fer 'im ter 'ave a good education. Now yer know why yer dad speaks proper English, not like me an' yer mum. But I could 'ave spoke betta if yer grandad 'ad found the time an' the patience ter learn me. But as I've said afower, I'm too old in the tooth ter start now. Any'ow, I must get on with the rest of me story.

'When yer dad was ten years old, Martha begun ter mek 'im a cake fer 'is birthday when she was took ill an' confined to 'er bed. I asked yer grandfather ter get a woman in ter 'elp me manage, an' one night 'e brought this Salvation Army wench 'ome with 'im. Martha took a dislike to 'er and so did I. She was noisy, bossy and behaved, as though 'er owned the place. He said if I dain't like 'er I could pack up an' clear out, an' tek me son as well!

'I put two an' two tergether and realised this was the wench 'e called Agnes an' was the reason fer the late nights. But I ignored 'im; I was content with me lot until I could save enough money ter leave 'im and tek me son with me.'

Grandma went on, 'One night I 'eard 'im quarrelin' with Ma in 'er bedroom an' 'eard 'im yell, "She'll tek her orders from me not you, an' if yer not satisfied yer can clear out an' all." "This is my house," I heard Ma reply, "an' be careful or yer might find yerself out *an'* that wench yer call Agnes, yer drunken womaniser!" I dain't ask wot the row was about in case 'e started on me, so I went in an' closed me bedroom door.'

'But, Grandma, you should have asked for your own peace of mind,' I said.

'I thought it best ter let Ma tell me sometime, but Ma was gettin' no betta, the doctor just gave 'er tablets ter kill the pains. Then one night when I was tryin' ter make 'er comfortable, I noticed Ma becum fidgety an' she began ter whisper, "Under me mattress you'll find a little box. Inside is ten gold sovereigns an' me death policy, I want yer to have them before I die." I told her not to talk like that an' that the Good Lord 'adn't got 'er name in the good book yet. I tried often ter cheer 'er up an' mek 'er comfortable, but I knew it was only a matter of time afower I was gooin' ter lose the best friend I ever 'ad.

'Then Ma went on ter say, "I got this feelin,' Hannah,

I ain't got long fer this wicked world or the people in it, so I want yer ter 'ave them." Then as she placed the sovereigns in the palm of me 'and and squeezed me fingers over them, she whispered agen, "'Ide 'em away, Hannah, where me son can't find 'em. I only wish there was more. Put 'em away till yer need em, Hannah, yer've bin a good daughter-in-law ter me, 'an when I goo ter me maker tek care of yerself an' me grandson, an' may God bless yer both.'"

Tears ran down my cheeks and my grandma's when she began to say, 'I told 'er not ter think about anythin', just ter lay down an' rest, an' that if that Agnes come ter disturb 'er I'd put 'er out in the street!'

Every night during the next week, while her husband was snoring Grandma would creep out of bed to see if Great-Grandma was comfortable or if she needed anything, but one night when she crept quietly into her bedroom she found that Ma had passed away in her sleep. She told me that Great-Grandma was buried in Witton Cemetery.

As usual, Grandma placed the bottle of embrocation on the hob to warm and I knew there would be no more questions until she was ready to continue.

Sometimes Grandma would be cheerful, other times very miserable, which I put down to the pain from her knees. Often I would hear her talking to herself as she sat in her rocking chair gazing into the fire. One dinner time, after we had had our rabbit and dumplings, I was clearing away the dishes when I heard her say, 'I'll 'ave ter finish 'em, I've only got 'alf a one ter do.'

When I asked her if she wanted anything she replied, 'It's me feet, luv, they get cold at night when me oven plate cools down. Will yer slip upstairs fer me, an' in me trunk beside me bed yer might find 'alf a sock I wanta finish.'

I looked in the trunk and was surprised to see several skeins of wool all tangled together, along with some half-finished small garments and one finished grey sock. As I gave her the half-knitted sock I said, 'Grandma, I didn't know you could knit.'

'There's a lot yer don't know about me yet,' she replied.

'Is all that wool yours, Grandma?' I asked.

'Whose do yer think it is? It ain't yer mum's 'cause I did all the knittin' fer yer when yer was all little babbies.'

'Mum never said.'

'No, I don't suppose 'er would, selfish bugger!' came Grandma's reply.

'I wish we could knit colourful things in school instead of that horrible khaki colour we have to use to knit scarves, socks an' balaclavas for the Tommies in France. One day I won first prize for the best knitted balaclava, Grandma,' I said proudly.

'Well, when the war's over yer can come an' unravel some o' that wool an' knit yerself summat useful.'

As I threw my arms round her and kissed her cheek, she said, 'Now, luv, I want yer ter goo ter the bake'ouse an' ask fer Mister Palmer. When 'e comes tell 'im yer've come fer Grandma's two penn'orth of yeast and a bag of flour. 'Ere's the sixpence, an' don't lose it! An' 'urry back out of the cold, I want ter get a loaf in the oven while I've gotta good fire underneath.'

When I arrived back from my errand I saw she was already standing by the table with the crock bowl ready. I watched her knead the bread and shape it into a cottage loaf, then place it in the oven. She sat back in her rocking chair as she wiped her hands down her apron, then opened her purse and gave me threepence to fetch a skein of grey wool.

I picked up my black beaded ta-ta purse inside of which was all I possessed: four pennies, five halfpennies and a few farthings I had saved from running errands for Mum's neighbours. The pennies I'd saved were the Saturday pocket money Dad gave each of us. I had eight-pence in all. I arrived at the little wool shop and asked the young woman behind the counter for a skein of grey wool for Grandma and two skeins of pink and a pair of wooden knitting pins for me. She told me the pink wool would be fourpence for one skein and twopence for a pair of knitting pins; this only left me with twopence. When I told her it was to begin knitting a shawl for Grandma, I was hoping she would let me have the other skein until I could bring her the twopence.

'I'm sorry, dear,' she said, 'but if you leave a deposit I will keep the wool for you, but only for one month. Now that'll be ninepence altogether,' she added.

'Thank you,' I replied, 'I'll be back before the month's up.' But what a lot of farthings I had to earn before I went back for that extra wool!

When I reached my grandma's she was over the fire poking hot coals under the oven. When she turned round and saw me she cried, 'Where've yer bin?' And as soon as she saw the pink colour, she said, 'I sent yer fer grey, not that colour!'

'I've get yer grey, but the pink's for me ter knit you a shawl instead of that faded cover off your bed,' I replied.

'That's very kind of yer, I'm glad ter 'ear somebody thinks about me.'

'I always do, I love you and my dad does,' I told her.

'I know, luv, and I know I'm a grumpy old woman at times, but I don't mean 'alf wot I say. Any'ow, I shall miss yer when yer goos back ter school.'

'I've still got tomorrow and the weekend, but I want to hear you talk some more about your life before then,' I replied, smiling.

'Yes, luv, I remember, but first I must get me bedsock finished after tea, I wanta wear 'em ternight afower me feet gets cold agen.'

The smell from the oven was making me feel hungry, and when the loaf was ready to be lifted out I asked if I could help, but she snapped back, 'Me 'ands are still useful, they're not crippled yet! Anyway, yer can lay the table fer me.'

I was never upset by her moods; she didn't mean to snap, she was in pain. I also knew how other people in our neighbourhood suffered, not only from pain but from the struggles, hardships and having too many mouths to feed.

I shall never forget that Friday afternoon when we sat down at the table and Grandma cut me a thick crust off her new warm loaf, spread with pure rosemary lard and pepper and salt. Although she taught me how to make bread, mine still never tastes the same as

Grandma's; even the lard bought today is not the same as when I used to fetch some from Stoddards pork butchers, where the pigs hung outside the shop. Oh how I miss Grandma's cooking and her home-made bread. That cheerful coal fire where we often sat together smiling and talking to the imaginary faces; each ember that fell would change to someone we knew or an animal we could recognise.

When we had had our fill and cleared away the dishes, Grandma said she would like to finish knitting her sock. I put the skein of wool on her outstretched hands and began to wind it into a ball. When this was finished she helped me with mine, and as we sat by the fire we both began to knit. I was too busy counting the stitches to ask her to tell me more of her life story, and Grandma was busy turning the heel of her sock, but as she got halfway along the foot I happened to look up and see her eyes closing, and when her knitting slipped on to her lap I knew she had dozed off. I knew she wanted it finished that night so I put my knitting away and picked up the sock. I had just finished casting off the toe when I saw her eyes slowly open and she asked, "Ow long 'ave I bin dozin' off?'

'Not long, Grandma, but I've finished yer sock.'

'Thank yer, luv, any'ow I feel betta after me forty winks,' she told me.

'Shall I make you a nice cup of tea and put some gin in, the kettle's already singing.'

'Yes, luv, but I don't think there's any gin left.'

'Well, me dad will be here to bring you a little bottle tomorrow,' I told her.

'What day is it then?' she cried out.

'It's Saturday tomorrow, Grandma,' I replied, smiling up at her.

'Oh yes, silly me, I must be getting forgetful,' she told me.

On Saturdays Dad would bring some vegetables, groceries and a small bottle of gin, together with some apples and oranges for me, and also my Saturday penny. Grandma couldn't eat an apple owing to only having two teeth, but when I gave her an orange she would love to suck it, or I would watch her take out a few slices and put them between bread and butter, which she called her 'orange snack'. Although I now have false teeth, I too enjoy an orange butty, just like my grandma made.

I saw her place the embrocation on the warm hob and start to rub her knees, and I knew it was time to put away my knitting. When I asked her if she wanted the oven plate put in her bed, she replied, 'Of cuss I do, an' me bedsocks.'

'My mum always says you get chilblains if you get your feet too hot, Grandma.'

'I've never 'ad 'em and I ain't likely ter get 'em at my age!' she replied.

I took off her canvas slippers, and after rolling down her thick, black woollen stockings I began to rub her knees.

'I fergot ter tell yer, luv, the doctor popped in ter see me while yer was gettin' me wool, an' when 'e took a look at me legs he told me 'e'd gotta come termorra an' visit Mrs Penny's daughter, an' 'ed bring me some more pills and some bandages ter be soaked in the embrocation and bound round me knees. Yo'll do that fer me won't yer, luv?'

'You know I will, Grandma,' I replied, 'but how will you manage when I have to go back home?'

Grandma said, 'Me neighbour next door, I know she'll oblige.'

'Well, if you do need me I'm sure my dad will let me come for an hour after school,' I told her.

By the time I had rubbed her knees and washed my hands it was almost time for our nightly mug of cocoa and to help Grandma to bed. After making her comfortable she said, 'I feel too tired ter tell yer any mower of the story, but I'll tell yer more after yer dad's bin an' gone.'

The following afternoon once the dinner dishes were cleared, we again sat facing each other by the fire and Grandma asked, 'Now, Katie, where did I finish the other night?' When I told her she said, 'Oh yes, I remember. Well, yer grandad seemed ter be settlin' down. He was still moody at times, but when 'e come from the Mission 'e seemed ter be more considerate. But after a few months, I saw a change in 'im. He began ter come 'ome late at night, sometimes 'e dain't come 'ome till the early 'ours. When I asked where 'e'd bin, 'ed say 'e 'ad ter stay be'ind an' do odd jobs fer the Captain. One night 'e dain't come 'ome at all, and when 'e walked in the next mornin' an' I asked 'im where 'e'd bin, 'e struck me twice across me face.

'When me neighbour saw me bruises she told me she 'ad seen 'im lots of times, arm in arm with that same Salvation Army wench wot used ter come ter the 'ouse when 'is Ma was alive. But when I med enquiries at the Mission they said they dain't want any scandal, but I knew they was coverin' up fer 'im. When 'e found out 'e began ter beat me agen.'

'But, Grandma! Why didn't you go to the police and tell them?' I asked.

'I did once, but all they said was they dain't interfere in family affairs. Any'ow, after that he packed all 'is bags an' left sayin' 'e was never comin' back an' fer two 'ole years I was content an' 'appy, an' even found a little part-time job cleanin' in an office. Durin' those two years me son left school ter find werk in London on a buildin' site, and once a month 'e would come 'ome and tek me out on walks or ter the pictures. I luved me son, Katie, but 'e 'ated is father an' swore wot 'e would do ter 'im if 'e ever saw 'im agen.

'One afternoon as I opened the door ter goo in, I couldn't believe me eyes. After two long years of peace an' 'appiness there 'e was sprawled out on the sofa drunk, 'e looked like a tramp. I just walked out the door agen an' went ter stay with me next-door neighbour. When I went back next mornin' I saw 'e was fryin' 'imself some eggs an' bacon over the fire. The first werds 'e spoke were "D'yer yer want some?" I dain't answer, but got meself a cuppa tea an' was gettin' meself ready ter goo ter werk when I 'eard 'im say, "You'll find yer bleedin' tongue when yer find out wots in store fer yer."

'I still dain't answer, I just walked out. When I cum back that afternoon I saw 'im sittin' by the fire readin' a newspaper an' I 'eard someone bangin' on the door. I opened it an' got another shock. Standing on the doorstep as brazen as yer like was that same young Salvation Army wench 'e'd bin carrying on with, an' a little lad about two years old an' a babby in arms. Before I could ask her wot she wanted, I 'eard 'im call out, "Come in, Agnes luv, an' bring the kiddies up ter the fire".

'I couldn't believe me ears, Katie, but as soon as I found me tongue I cried out, "Wot's gooin' on 'ere?", an' when 'e said they was ter mek their 'ome with us, I yelled out, "Oh no they ain't!", but 'e said they was 'is two children an' 'is 'ouse an' if I dain't like it I could clear out.'

'But, Grandma, what did she have to say to all of this?' I asked.

'She just sat by the fire warmin' 'er legs, an' as she pulled out 'er breast ter feed the babby I saw the smirk on 'er face. I knew then that this must 'ave been arranged between 'em for sometime. I couldn't get out o' that 'ouse quick enough. As soon as I'd packed a few clothes in a bag I walked towards the door and yelled out, "If yer think I'm gooin' ter stay 'ere an' be a lackey fer yo and yer whore an' yer two bastards, yer'll 'ave ter think agen!"'

'Oh, Grandma, did you really use that language?' I asked.

'I'm sorry, luv, I couldn't think of anythin' else ter say, I was so shocked an' angry with 'em. That 'ad been the only real 'ome I'd ever known, while Ma was alive, now I dain't know where I was 'eading' for, but sooner than goo back an' live with 'em I would 'ave walked the streets or gone in the workhouse!

'I stood on the corner of the street wonderin' which way ter turn when one of me neighbours asked why I was weepin'. When I tried ter explain she kindly said she would put me up until I found a place of me own. But I wanted ter get miles away an' start a new life fer meself an' me son when 'e come back at the end of the month. Any'ow, Katie, I still 'ad them gold sovereigns Ma give me afower she died, also some o' the money me son sent me once a month. But it only wanted three wicks before 'e would be back agen, so I 'ad ter find a place fer us both.

'That same mornin' I caught the tram an' found meself in the Hockley Brook district, but landlords wanted the earth fer furnished rooms. I walked up Pitsford Street an' then found meself in Vyse Street where I saw an empty, dilapidated old Georgian 'ouse ter let, facing Warstone Cemetery.'

The area my grandma was describing to me then was where all my family once lived and where I was born, but these old bug-infested Georgian houses no longer exist today. Vyse Street and the surrounding districts now make up the very fashionable Jewellery Quarter. But I still remember those districts and houses that were more like rabbit warrens, where crowded families of two or three generations tried to exist.

Grandma went on to say that she saw an elderly woman swilling outside her door and asked her how much the rent of the empty house was. The woman replied, 'It's four shillin' a wick, but that's the best one around 'ere, all the others are a half-crown a wick. Any'ow,' she added, 'it's got two bedrooms, and if yer interested the keys are a tanner to look over it. I could do with it meself with my brood, but I carn't afford that rent, yer see a couple o' bob goes a long way when yer got too many 'ungry mouths ter feed.'

Grandma said that when she went inside and looked around she saw dust and cobwebs everywhere. There was a large front room, a kitchen, a scullery with a back door leading to the cobbled yard where several occupied houses faced each other and where many ragged children of all ages were playing tic-tac around the lamp-post. 'Them children looked scared when they saw me, Katie, an' ran indoors, an' as I looked across the yard I saw the usual brewhouse an' dry closets and water stand pipe. I saw women and children of all ages come on their doorsteps ter see who I was, and when I went back inside the house I knew that with a bit of spit, polish an' elbow grease, the 'ouse 'ad possibilities. I bought second-'and furniture an' other goods an' utensils I needed. I was determined ter mek this an 'ome fer meself an' me son, an' thanked the good Lord that I was young an' strong. Three weeks later, when everythin' was ship-shape, I went ter the station ter meet me son.

'When I told 'im wot 'ad 'appened, an' why I was livin' in Vyse Street, 'e went ter see 'is father the next day, but when 'e come 'ome, 'e said the 'ouse was empty an' up fer sale.'

'Did you know where they went or why?' I asked.

'We never did know, an' we never saw or 'eard of 'em agen. When Sam come back from London ter werk fer a firm in the Midlands I was happy ter be cookin' an' doin' fer both of us or whatever was needed.

'Saturday afternoons we'd stroll around the Bull Ring

an' buy our vegetables from the barra' boys, an' later
'ave a drink in the Nelson, but each night after 'e come
'ome from work, 'e'd wash an' shave an' put 'is suit on an'
then goo to our local, the George an' Dragon. Sometime
later I was told 'e'd been seen out with a barmaid. When
I asked 'im why he 'adn't told me, 'e said 'e'd bring 'er
'ome ter meet me. As soon as I saw 'er I knew there was
somethin' about 'er I dain't like. It wasn't the paint an'
powder she used on 'er face, nor because she was igno-
rant an' illiterate, for I'd 'ad the same experience as a
young girl, but at least I did try ter betta meself, Katie.
Sam told me that she was two months pregnant an' they
were gettin' married. 'E asked me if they could live with
me until they found a place of their own. When the
babby was stillborn, I knew she'd lied ter me about how
many months pregnant 'er was, but when 'er began ter
cry I said I would keep 'er secret.

'But Katie, I couldn't tolerate 'er slovenly 'abits, an'
when she began ter 'ave one child after another an' I
looked after 'em while they were out drinkin', an' then
they'd come back quarrelin', I told 'em both they would
'ave ter get a place of their own ter live. In the next few
days they found a back-to-back and that's where you,
Frankie an' Liza was born. But afower you were born yer
dad fell outta work and went ter the Boer War. When 'e
come back there was no work fer anybody. Times were
'ard, 'an when the landlords put up their rent it was too
'igh ter pay, 'an families let off their rooms ter far an' near
ter start a small business makin' cheap jewellery. They
were paying a few shillin's ter the tenants, but crafty landlords 'ad their eye ter business too. The rents rose ter

that extreme it was impossible fer poor people ter pay. I was lucky ter find this back-ter-back house where I am today, but many defenceless people with young families were given notice to quit or 'ad the bailiffs.

'Some moved ter other areas ter live with parents or neighbours, or did a moonlight flit, but the elderly or infirm were turned out into the streets or work'ouse. It wasn't long afower these old Georgian 'ouses sprang up ter become known as the Jewellery Quarter. Yer family were lucky, Katie, ter be livin' in a back-ter-back alley-way which no one was interested in.'

Sunday morning was my last day to be with Grandma before I went back home to get ready to start school again. As soon as I came downstairs I made a pot of tea and then went back upstairs to help Grandma dress, but she was still asleep. After laying the table, I again went back upstairs and saw her trying to get herself out of bed. When I asked if she was all right I heard her mumble, 'Leave me a bit, Katie, I'll be all right, don't worry none.'

But as I helped her dress and go downstairs, and saw her flop into her rocking chair, I noticed how pale she was. I didn't know she was ill until she asked me to tell the next-door neighbour to come in. When I knocked on the door Mrs Penny said she was very sorry but she couldn't come yet as her daughter-in-law was in labour. I ran all the way home but my mother made some excuse that she had to get the washing done before it rained; the sun was shining and there wasn't a dark cloud anywhere, so I said how ungrateful and selfish she was. Before I could say more she slapped me twice across the face with the back of her hand.

There was nothing I could do but run back to Grandma's where I saw several of her neighbours wiping their eyes on their aprons. When I asked what was wrong Mrs Penny said Grandma was dead. I ran back home to tell my mother, but all she said was, 'Now we'll 'ave ter find the policies an' get 'er buried.' I never forgave my mother for those harsh, cruel words.

The last time I saw my lovable old grandma was in candle light as she lay peacefully in her coffin beneath the window with the paper blind pulled down. I never did finish that pink shawl.

As the years rolled by I began to miss my grandma more than ever. Often I would think of those sunny afternoons going for walks and ending up near the sand pits in Goodman Street recreation grounds, where she would push me on the swings. On our way home she would call at Stoddards where the pigs hung outside, and buy chitterlings, tripe or a pig's trotter for our supper and, after that, we would pull up our chairs to the fire and watch for strange faces in the flames. There was nothing better than a coal fire to welcome you home after a cold evening out, and to toast a piece of bread on the wire fork and then spread it with dripping.

St Paul's Church was where I was baptised ninety-seven years ago, in 1903, as were many of my brothers and sisters, and other babies living in the district. But St Paul's was really for the gentry who had money to buy a seat, and the graveyard was also for gentry only; poor people were buried in Warstone Lane Cemetery in communal graves, and when we had to attend church on Sundays we were pushed into the gallery.

Although my sister Liza had to attend Sunday service with us, she never came to play with us in the churchyard. She always used to say it was wicked to chase around the tombstones and to play on consecrated ground. I was afraid to mention the ribbon she stole from wreaths to adorn her hair.

Saturdays were usually the best time to play in the churchyard, when our Vicar was in the local pub. Everyone knew he liked his whisky and was often seen carrying a bottle beneath his frock.

One Friday afternoon as soon as I came home from school, Mum was waiting on the doorstep. When she saw me she called, ''Urry yerself, I want yer ter fetch me an errand!'

'Why can't Liza go? I'm tired and I ran all the way from school.'

She slapped my face. 'You'll do as yer told! I want yer ter goo or else.' That 'or else' meant many things as punishment, and she never forgot when I refused.

The following Saturday afternoon I fetched my go-cart up from the cellar and placed it in the side entry while I went to fetch the little kids, but when I came back it was missing. I looked all over the house. Thinking my mum had carried out her threat, I even looked down the cellar again. Had she hidden it away ready to burn it later because I disobeyed her? I dared not ask her because I knew she would lie to me and I'd get a belting into the bargain. I sat down in the entry and began to cry. I had lost the only thing I enjoyed.

After a while I stood up and wiped my eyes on my pinafore. I enquired from door to door, but no one had seen it. The last door I knocked at was at the bottom of the entry. As soon as Mrs Brannon appeared I told her what had happened and asked if she had seen anyone take it, but she said she hadn't. As I began to cry again, she said, 'Never mind, luv. If I see it or find out who's got it, I'll tell yer.'

'No one's ever taken it before, Mrs Brannon. I've had it for a long time and I've promised Mrs Taylor's twins and little Billy Floyd to take them a ride.'

'Well, wipe yer eyes an' yer can 'ave the loan of me bassinet for a penny. Promise yer won't damage it, 'cos I need it for me kids ter fetch the coal from the wharf. I'll wheel it out from the brew'ouse.'

When I saw it I wondered if I would be able to wheel it. It was a high-sided relic on four wheels with two ragged hoods on each end of the seats. In the centre was a well containing a cracked and stained chamber pot and several rags. I thanked her and wheeled it away but the smell from it made me feel sick. As I stood it outside our door, I thanked God no one was at home. I had another look to see if Mum had hidden my cart, but it was nowhere to be seen. I even had another look down the cellar, hoping she had thrown it down there while I was out.

I could not disappoint the little kids expecting their ride so I helped myself to some of Mum's disinfectant (Condy's Fluid was supplied free by the council), and poured a drop in the pot and the well of the bassinet before returning the bottle and going to collect the twins and little Bobby Floyd. When their mother saw me pushing this old battered contraption, she asked, 'Wherever 'ave yer got that from? The rag-and-bone yard?'

'No, Mrs Taylor,' I managed to reply. 'Mrs Brannon has lent it to me until me cart comes to light.'

'Well, I 'ope yer find it, 'cos I don't think any of the kids would steal it. Did that old skinflint charge yer a penny?'

'No, Mrs Taylor. I told her I hadn't got one so she lent it to me for nothin'.'

''Er must be gettin' generous in 'er old age,' she replied. 'Anyway, 'ere's the twins an' Bobby, so be careful 'ow yer goo. If yer carn't manage just bring 'em back. I'll understand 'cos they ain't bin well.'

'I'll manage, Mrs Taylor.'

After she had lifted the twins on to one seat and little Bobby on to the seat opposite, I began my journey with them sucking their dummies. But I hadn't gone far when Joey was sick all down his little frock and all over his twin, and Bobby began to cry. There was nothing I could wipe the vomit up with and the only rags in the pram were still wet from the Condy's Fluid, so I took off my pinafore. As I began to wipe their faces there was an awful smell and a breaking of wind and I realised little Bobby had filled his trousers. I lifted him out to clean him up and another squirt came from him and on to the outside of the bassinet. This was too much, I lost my temper and slammed him back on to the seat and wheeled them all back home.

When I saw Mrs Taylor I started to explain but began

to cry. She told me it was her fault really and that she had been up half the night with them.

When I asked her why she let me take them out she replied, 'Well, I thought the fresh air might do 'em good. Never mind, luv. Gi'mme yer pinny and I'll get it washed an' I'll tek the bassinet back fer yer.'

I vowed then that that would be last time I would ever take anyone's kids out again until I found my cart. But I never did, and I still believe to this day that my mother carried out her threat.

For King and Country

I was nearly twelve years of age when, one afternoon on my way home from school, I saw several men talking in groups and shaking their heads. This was unusual as the streets were normally quiet at that time of day. As I hurried home I saw Mum and several of our neighbours gossiping at the end of the yard. Again I couldn't understand this as she usually had no time for neighbours and so I knew it must be serious. When I got close enough I heard Mrs Owens say, 'It's true, Polly. Me lodgers come 'ome early ter tell me.'

'Mary, Mother of God!' Mrs Flynn cried out as she began to cross herself. 'What's ter become of me and me babies?'

"Don't fret yerself, it's only rumours,' Mrs Freer comforted her. 'Any'ow, I ain't got me no 'usband, so it won't bother me one way or another.'

Suddenly I heard Mum cry, 'Well, I got me an 'usband

an' two grown sons an' I'm sure I ain't goin' ter let them fight in no bleedin' war! Not if I can 'elp it! Any'ow, my Sam done 'is whack for the Queen in the Boer War and what thanks did 'e get? Stabbed in the neck and still got the scar to show for it!'

'Anyway, it might only be rumours,' Mrs Taylor emphasised.

'Let's 'ope it is!' Mum piped up. 'I'm more bothered about gettin' me washin' out afower it rains.'

As soon as the neighbours broke up and Mum and Mrs Mitchell went into the brewhouse, I went indoors. When I saw Liza and Frankie, I asked, 'Is it true, Frankie? Are we going to be at war with Germany?'

'I don't know, Katie, but I did hear rumours and our head master has cut our lessons to tell us more about history, including the Austrians and the Germans, and the Zulus and the Boers.'

'But there ain't any Boers left,' Liza chimed in.

'Don't you believe it!' Frankie exclaimed. 'Our head master told all the boys there will always be wars as long as there's greedy nations.'

'I hope our dad don't have ter go agen,' I thought aloud.

'I don't know, Katie. I hope not now he's got a regular job, especially when he did his bit in the Boer War,' Frankie said.

Suddenly Liza volunteered, 'I 'ope 'e does and never comes back!'

Frankie caught hold of her and hit her so hard she fell to the floor. 'Now tell yer mum wot yer've just said ter me, if yer dare, yer wicked bugger!'

'Pick me up, me 'eads bleedin'!' she yelled.

'Get yerself up! And I hope yer never ferget what yer've just said!'

When I bent down to help her, Frankie cried, 'Leave her there, the wicked sod! She can get 'erself up unless she wants ter lie there and explain ter Mum why.'

My two elder brothers Jack and Charlie were not living at home. Jack was living across the street with a woman whose husband was away in the Regular Army, and Charlie was lodging with his workmate and his mother. By now Mary was married with three children and her husband was a Regular soldier too.

One day I came home and saw them all huddled over the crackling wireless. Dad jumped up and exclaimed, 'I bloody well told 'em, but no one listened ter me!'

'Anyway,' Jack replied, 'I've heard it'll all be over in six months. Dad, can yer lend me a tanner?'

'Why should I, yer dain't pay me back the last couple of bob I lent yer. What's it for?'

'I want to go to the George for a drink and a couple of packets of Woodbines.'

'Why don't yer buy yerself a clay pipe and two penn'orth of twist. It's cheaper. Anyway, if yer like ter wait for me I'll get me coat and come with yer.'

'But Sam!' Mum objected. 'Ye've gotta get back ter work.'

'It can wait. I don't think there'll be much done terday now they've 'eard the news.'

'But they wun't need yo now ter fight, Sam, will they? Yo done yower bit in the Boer War and yer got a regular job now.'

'Job or no job, Polly, I'm too old. But if I'm needed I'll have ter go,' Dad told her.

'But what thanks did yer get, Sam? Thrown out of work and tryin' ter exist on what we could scrounge like thousands of other families. 'Er never bothered 'er 'ead about 'er people, an' yo a sergeant an' all!'

'It made no difference what yer rank was, Polly, and it wasn't all Queen Victoria's troubles. But I'll ter yer this much – and you, Jack and Charlie – if the politicians weren't so greedy lining their pockets while they sat on their fat arses arguing, there might never be wars,' Dad said angrily.

'Well,' said Jack, 'nothing ain't goin' ter stop me from joining up.'

'Yer better think twice, son. Don't be too eager. Wait and see what happens first.'

'But I'm outa work and there's nothing for me ter stay here for. I could do with the King's shilling.'

'And me,' Charlie added.

'Not you, Charlie,' Mum cried as she began to wipe her tears.

'They won't take 'im, Polly. He's only seventeen.'

'Well, I'll join up when I'm eighteen an' nobody ain't gooin' ter stop me!' Charlie told them firmly.

'Don't be young fools the pair of yer!' Dad exclaimed. 'Yer don't know what a war can do ter yer. It's no bleedin' holiday camp, sleeping rough in all kinds of weather, and it'll be no use yer thinkin' of leavin' when yer've 'ad enough. I've seen good men stood against a wall in front of a firing squad and shot! Yer better go an' 'ave yer pint and think it over. I'll see yer later.'

Soon after, Dad slipped on his coat and left to join the neighbours as they hurried towards the local pub to listen to the rest of the news broadcast over the wireless as they supped their pints of ale.

I saw tears in my sister's eyes as she said, 'I'll have ter be going now, Mum. I'm expecting a letter from Albert.'

'All right, luv. Per'aps 'e'll tell yer more news.'

Mary's husband was a sergeant with the South Staffordshire Regiment. His letters used to come regularly once a week, but she had been worried for some time as they were now few and far between. One day she was expecting him home on leave and all the family got together to greet him, but she received a short letter to say the leave had been cancelled and the Regiment would soon be shipped over to France.

My brother Jack ended up stationed at Aldershot in the Royal Field Artillery. As soon as my brother Charlie heard he tried to join up too, but the recruiting officer saw he'd altered the date on his birth certificate and turned him away. A few weeks later he tried another recruiting office where he had more luck with the old veterans. As soon as Mum found out she marched over there and told them that Charlie was under age, but the old veterans only laughed at her and told her to go home. Mum would have the last word, however. 'All yo old men just want our sons for bleeding gun fodder, an' by the look on yer it would be better if yer got up and went 'ome yerself. That's if yer can walk that far, yer dodderin' ole fools.' She was still yelling and crying when a policeman came to escort her away to Kenyon Street Police Station.

Dad went with the rent book to bail her out, only to find that she had already been tried and fined half a crown for disturbing the peace. Dad paid the fine but told the Magistrate that if she got into more trouble he would leave her there.

Many factories and small firms which had been closed down for a long period due to lack of orders were opening up again and booming, making shells, guns, bullets and all kinds of armaments. Now there were plenty of jobs for everyone, but as all the young and able men were at war in France, women and young girls were employed, working all hours with little sleep. Money was now plentiful, but there was talk of food rationing.

Even us girls at school did our bit for the 'Tommies' (as our soldiers were often called). Our classes were changed around now for those girls aged ten upwards. We were taught to knit khaki scarves, balaclavas and socks. Socks were always knitted on four pins, which teachers often came to inspect, and if we had dropped a stitch we were severely caned and made to unravel it all and start again from scratch. When the socks were finished and perfect we were told to write a cheery little message and fold it inside each sock.

My friend Winnie wrote, 'Come home soon, Tommy, and God bless and watch over you, love Winnie.' Other notes were similar. I wrote, 'I love you, brave Tommy, and will ask you to marry me when you return. God bless from Katie. xx.'

Each message was read by our head teacher before it was passed. Some she passed, but others she would frown at and tear up. Winnie and I kept our fingers crossed, and when we saw her smile we knew we were all right.

The day I was fourteen I was called into the head teacher's office where I was presented with a book called *Alice in Wonderland*, along with my good conduct certificate and a lecture which I also remember.

'Now, Kate, I want you to listen carefully to what I have to say,' she began.

Nervously I stood looking up at her, waiting and wondering.

'Now you are leaving us I wish you well, dear, but I also warn you that you will be starting another life from now on in which there are different lessons to be learned. If at any time you wish to come and see us, we will be glad to see you. Also, I wish you to keep on the straight and narrow way of life, as we have taught many girls who often come to see us on a visit. Do you understand what I am trying to tell you, dear?'

'Yes, miss,' I replied.

She gave me my certificate of merit and my prize, kissed my cheek, and as she shook my hand said, 'God bless you, child.' I felt tears come into my eyes.

I have never forgotten those words of wisdom. As soon as I closed the school room door behind me for the last time, I opened my prize and there on the flyleaf in gilt letters were the words:

Presented to: Kate Greenhill
For Good Conduct
At Camden Grove Church School
Signed by Agnes D. Ford – February 1st, 1917
Head Teacher

It was a wet, bitterly cold day as I hurried home with my treasures beneath my shabby brown coat. I arrived indoors to see Mum stirring up the fire with the poker. As I made to go upstairs with my treasures she turned around. 'What yer got there? Mower rubbish?'

When I told her, she said, 'Well, yer betta 'urry yerself. I want some coal brought up from the cellar.'

When I had done that I asked, 'Do you know what day it is, Mum?'

'Yes! What about it?' she snapped.

'It's my birthday, Mum, I'm fourteen,' I cried out excitedly.

'Well, yo'll be able ter earn yer keep now.'

'When?' I asked eagerly.

'Monday mornin' I'm tekin yer to a factory where they'll pay the best wages.'

'But I can go on me own now. I've got me birth certificate.'

'Yo gotta be examined and passed by a doctor fust, an' that's gonna cost me a tanner!'

'But the doctor at the school clinic said I was fit.'

'Don't keep mitherin' me! Yo've still gotta 'ave a note ter prove yer fit, so when yer've 'ad yer bath, I'm tekin yer ter see the doctor. Now get yer grub down yer and 'elp me get the bath off the wall.'

When we had dragged the heavy galvanised bath on to the hearth in front of the fire, Mum began to empty two heavy kettles of boiling water into it and then added some cold. I stood watching her as she poured in Condy's Fluid. She pushed a piece of carbolic soap in my hand and yelled in my ear, 'Come on, get in! I ain't got all day ter see ter yo!'

As I got into the milky water I began to squirm, even my little fanny felt on fire, but I knew if I cried out I would get more. When she began to rub my back with the soap I felt worse. She had a habit of rough handling at the best of times, but I didn't deserve this. When it was over I dried myself with the hessian towel; I was still tingling all over and my body was as red as a lobster's!

I managed to get dressed and helped empty the bath and hang it back on the outside wall. Now I was ready for Mum to take me to the doctor's, where he gave me a bottle of Parish's Food and the note I needed.

My first job was also my first experience of a factory. Nicklins made munition parts for outworkers. It was noisy and dirty and women of all ages wore khaki overalls and funny looking headgear, like a chef's hat. The first task I was given was helping an old lady called Fanny to sweep the oily floors and make tea for the ones who worked on the power presses. I thought it was terrible to call this old dear Fanny as I knew this word was used to refer to a female's private parts.

One day I asked her what her real name was.

'Frances 'Iggins, but we all 'ave nicknames or numbers 'ere.'

'But don't yer mind being called Fanny?'

'I don't mind what they call me as lung as they don't call me too late for me dinner!' came her reply.

'What do yer think they'll call me?'

'Key 'ole Kate, if yer goo around askin' questions,' she answered, smiling.

'I'll remember,' I replied, as I sat on the three-legged oily stool waiting for the urn to boil.

'Yer betta not let the foreman see yer sittin' down. 'E's comin' over,' Fanny whispered.

He stood in front of me. 'Who told *you* you could sit down?'

'I ain't doing any harm. I'm tired and I'm waiting for the water to boil,' I replied.

'Well, when you've made the tea I want to see you in my office!' he exclaimed.

As he walked away Fanny warned, 'Watch yerself, Kate. With that smirk of 'is, 'es very plausible.'

'I've been taught ter use me knee,' I replied.

I made my way up two flights of narrow stairs and he must have heard my footsteps because he called out, 'No need ter knock, me dear. Come on in.'

As I entered, I felt the heat from the small room he called his office. There was an overpowering smell of stale beer and tobacco smoke. I had never really looked at him before, but as he sat behind his untidy desk with his greasy shirt wide open, I thought how ugly he looked.

His hair was plastered down with Brylcreem and he needed a shave. There were grey hairs growing down from his nostrils and out of his ears and a thick mass of black hair on his chest. He reminded me of Weary Willie, the tramp I'd read about in Frankie's comics.

When he got up and walked towards me I felt very nervous. ''Ow old did yer say yer was?'

'I didn't, sir.'

'Well, 'ow old are yer, luv?' he asked.

'I'm fourteen, sir.'

'Yer sure yer not older?' came his reply.

'No, sir.'

'Well, yer a big wench fer fourteen. Turn round and let's see yer properly.'

As I turned around I could feel his eyes undressing me. I was willing to use my knee if he dared touch me. As I opened the office door to leave, he said, 'I wanta see yer on Friday, and from now on yer ter call me Tom.'

'Yes, sir,' I replied, with a touch of sarcasm.

I fled down those stairs as though the devil were after me. When I got to the bottom, out of breath, I felt everyone's eyes on me. When I told Fanny what had happened, she replied, 'I'm sorry, luv, but I dain't 'ave time ter warn yer. He tries it on with all the young girls 'e fancies but they either ignore 'im or leave.'

'Well, there's one here who's going ter leave!' I told her.

'I don't blame yer, luv, but yer want ter watch out fer blokes like 'im wherever yer work. Now come on, let's get on with cleanin' the closets.' These were real closets with running water, not like the dry closets we shared with the neighbours. As we stood in the passage with our mops and buckets Fanny said, 'Katie, I couldn't talk ter yer properly while some of the women were watchin', but I want ter give yer a bit of advice. Whenever it's time ter fall in love with a feller, remember, never let them interfere with yer till yer sure that ring's on yer finger ter stay, or you'll be in disgrace for the rest of yer life. You understand what I'm tryin' ter say?' she added.

'Yes, Mrs Higgins.'

'I know. I ain't always been a dried-up old woman. I was very attractive once. Fellers used ter 'ang around me like bees round a jam pot, but the life I led through the stress and poverty years soon told on me.'

'Ain't yer got any family or husband?'

'No, luv. My Bertie was killed in the Boer War, an' when I become destitute I took in men lodgers. Later when they left I 'ad ter find somethin' else and now I'm only fit ter be a lackey for other people.'

I felt so sad when I saw tears in her eyes, but after she wiped them away, she asked, ''Ave you got any parents, luv?'

'Yes, my dad and my mum.'

'Well, if yer listen to their wise words and foller their advice, yer wun't go far wrong. That's what I should 'ave done when I was yer age. Now let's finish mopping the closets before I start weepin' again.'

As soon as Friday night came and I was paid, I slipped half a crown in her apron pocket and kissed her goodbye. I never told my mother I had left my job or why. I don't think she would have believed me anyway. I gave her the ten shillings from my wage packet, then with the two shillings I had left bought myself fish and chips and a bag of scratchings. After satisfying my hunger, I made my way next door to our local Lyric Picture House, where I treated myself to one of the best seats. I still had change from my two shillings to treat my brother to a seat in the 'gods' on Saturday afternoon.

The Metropole Theatre was situated in Snow Hill and was often called 'the blood tub' or 'the flea pit'; children were only allowed in on Saturday afternoon, unless they were with an adult.

We never told Mum about our little secret, otherwise it would have meant we had to have Liza with us.

As soon as Monday morning came, I took Mum her usual cup of tea upstairs, and after putting on my *Daily Mail* stockings and boots, I ate my meagre breakfast. I put my lunch of bread and potted meat (which Mum had cut up the night before) into a paper bag, slipped on my long shabby brown coat, and closing the door behind me I went out to find another job.

I walked up and down several streets trying to keep warm for it was a bitterly cold day, when at last I came to Victoria Street (still in the Jewellery Quarter). A notice outside the Brass Works said: 'Young girls wanted to learn press work'. I climbed the stairs and rang the bell. A buxom woman appeared dressed in a white overall. Straight away I said, 'I've come in answer to the notice outside.'

She asked all the usual questions, name, address, but when she asked my age I told a little white lie and said I was fifteen. She seemed pleased and so was I when she told me my wages would be sixteen shillings a week and I could start that same afternoon. But I was eager to start right away otherwise I would have to while away the morning feeling cold.

When I asked if I could start right away, she wanted to know why I was so keen.'

'Well, I'll have to walk about until two o'clock and I'm very cold,' I told her.

'I'm sorry, dear. It will still have to be two o'clock and don't be late because the gates close when the hooter stops.'

I felt a little disappointed as I made my way down the stairs, but as I walked along Warstone Lane I saw a little coffee shop which I entered and had a cup of tea and a bun. It was nearly ten o'clock so I still had four hours to go. After another cup of tea with loads of sugar, I took a brisk walk towards St Pauls churchyard where I sat on a bench to watch the pigeons. I was hoping that soon the Vicar or the church warden would open the doors to the church, but unfortunately no one came.

I knew I had to stay on the move to keep warm, so I made my way into New Street where I saw several well-dressed women making their way towards the Kardomah coffee house. I knew if I were to go in there and order a cup of coffee they would look down on me. But why shouldn't I? I'm as good as they are. Maybe they had forgotten *their* childhood upbringings.

I plucked up my courage and as I entered I saw the waitress look me up and down. I didn't think she was going to serve me until I smiled at her and said in my best tone, 'One cup of coffee, dear, with cream and sugar.' As she slapped it down on the counter, I smiled again, picked up the cup of coffee and boldly sat myself down. Heads turned to stare as I sat sipping my coffee with my little finger cocked. I stared back and was pleased to see that now they ignored me. It seemed heavenly to sit on a plush chair in the warmth of that coffee house and, after ordering two more cups of coffee, I stayed until it was time to leave. As I walked outside I smiled to myself and wondered what they were all saying and thinking of me.

The forewoman met me at the works entrance and gave me a clocking-in card and I followed her into a large workshop, which looked the same as the one I had already left.

There were noisy power presses and hand machines where women and girls were working. The floors were oily, and even the stairs and stools were black with grease.

I was told to call her 'Madam' and my first jobs were sweeping up swarf and making tea. I did these jobs for almost two weeks, the wages were good and the workers were very helpful. One morning Madam came to tell me that I was to have a change and I would be cutting brass strips of metal on a guillotine.

'But I've never worked a guillotine, Madam,' I replied.

'Now's your time to learn.' She handed me a khaki overall and a large hat which kept falling over my eyes. When she saw the trouble I was having with it she said, 'If you cut some of that hair off you'll be able to see better!'

'Cut me hair off, my mum would kill me!' I replied.

'Like that, is it? Well, here's a safety pin. Make a tuck in it because we don't want you to have an accident.'

I watched as she used her foot to push along a large roll of brass towards the guillotine, then after showing me how the foot lever worked, I began to cut the metal into strips two feet long.

'If you're in any trouble, one of the women will help you.'

After the strips were ready I had to carry them to a power press where I waited until they were cut and shaped into small round discs. My next job was to collect them and take them to the drilling machine, where I had to drill in four holes. How proud I was when I was told these were now brass buttons for soldiers' trousers and that I was doing my bit towards the war effort.

Whenever I had a thicker gauge of metal to cut, the lever of the guillotine always gave my feet cramp. Once when I bent down to rub them, I found Madam bending over me. I expected her to replace me but she just walked away. Next thing I knew she had fetched in another girl from one of the other workshops to help me.

'This is Lizzie Farrell!' she barked. 'She's to help you in future, to cut, carry and whatever to the power press workers, and no talking or whispering! Can you both read?' she asked, pointing to the notice board. 'Right,' she added as we both nodded our heads. 'Otherwise it's instant dismissal, a fine or both!' As she walked away we both made signs with our hands and eyes. From that day forward Lizzie and I became close friends.

She was two years older than me and we were both the same height but not the same build. Lizzie was well developed and also very good looking, with fair shoulder-length wavy hair; she also had the biggest blue eyes I'd ever seen, a lovely fair complexion and a good figure, and she knew it too. I was quite the reverse, I had round oval features, straight black hair, dark blue eyes and a sallow complexion; I was also slim. I was never envious of her figure. I knew that one day when I was older my little titties would start to develop, and until then I stuffed cotton wool down my corset to try to compete. One day my mother caught me and threw them on the fire and, as I watched them burn, she slapped my face.

Listening to the way Lizzie spoke of her life often reminded me of my mum. I wondered if her mum was like mine.

One Saturday morning I was surprised to see my brother waiting for me to come out of the works. 'Frankie,' I cried out. 'What are you doing here?'

'I've been waitin' ter see yer. I've got somethin' ter tell yer.'

'Why can't it wait till I get home? I'm waiting for Lizzie Farrell.'

'I have ter tell yer now before Mum finds out.'

'Is this another one of your jokes?' I asked, smiling.

'It's nothing ter smile about, I'm serious!'

'All right then, spit it out.'

'Well, this morning Mum told me ter fetch the boiler stick from the brewhouse.'

'Why? Who's she going to use it on this time?'

'Yer think I'm joking don't yer,' he said, and when I saw the serious look on his face, I replied, 'Go on then.'

"Well, Mum said she dain't want ter leave it there for somebody else ter use it, so I went ter get it.'

'When I got ter the brewhouse I saw smoke comin' out under the door, I tried ter push it open but it seemed wedged. When I did get in who do you think was behind it? Our Liza and that funny-lookin' wench she calls George, smoking cigarettes. And hiding behind the mangle was Tommy Freer! Before I could say anything they fled, nearly knocked me over and that's the truth!'

'Have you told Mum?'

'No, not yet. I've been tryin' ter get summat on Liza for a long time and now I've found 'er out!'

"Well, now you've caught her, I think you had better tell Mum.'

'Not yet, Katie.'

'But why not?'

'You know yerself she wouldn't believe me or you. Whatever we said about 'er, Mum thinks the sun shines out of 'er arse! But she won't lie 'er way out of this. When I find out where she's got the money ter buy fags, then I'll tell Mum!'

'How are you going to find out?'

'I'm gooin' ter do a bit of detective work.'

'Can I help?'

'No, Katie. I'll do it on me own when there's no one else in the house. It might be this afternoon when Mum and Liza go to the meat market.'

'Well, best of luck, Frankie,' I told him. 'It's about time she had her comeuppance!'

As he went to walk away, I called out, 'Want ter come to the Met with us?'

'Who yer mean by us?' he asked.

'Me and my work mate, Lizzie Farrell.'

'Not now,' he replied.

'All right, perhaps next Saturday,' I said.

'I've already seen *The Clutching Hand* at the Lyric, twice. And yer better not let Mum know yer goin' ter the flea pit. Remember how she thrashed us when Liza wet the bed? Well, ta-ra fer now,' he called back as he made his way home.

I shall never forget those thrashings Mum gave us when Liza blamed us for wetting the bed. Nor could I ever understand why she never said sorry she had beaten us when she found out the truth.

When we came out of the theatre, I was surprised to see Frankie waiting outside. 'Hello, Katie,' he said. 'I've bin waitin' ter tell yer something private.'

'Don't be too long or I'll get a wallopin' off me mum,' said Lizzie.

'It can wait. I don't want yer friend ter get in trouble,' Frankie said. 'Any'ow I'll tell yer when we're on our own.'

'Is it serious?' I asked.

'Yes, yer'll be surprised when I tell yer all right. See yer later.'

As he walked away I hurried to catch up with Lizzie. When she saw me she asked, 'Is that one of yer boyfriends?'

'No, it's only Frankie.'

'Frankie? An' who's Frankie?' she asked.

'He's me brother,' I told her.

'Nice looker too, ain't 'e?' she smiled.

'If he hears yer say that you'll have him blushin', and he's got a paddy too!'

'Well,' she said. 'Yer can introduce me to 'im sometime.'

'Come on, Lizzie,' I told her. 'You've got plenty of boyfriends to brag about, and what's the last one's name you told me about?'

'Yer mean Percy Timmins? 'E ain't me regular, well not yet, I'm feelin' me way befower I get serious.'

Misunderstanding what she meant, I cried, 'What yer mean feeling yer way?'

'I don't mean what yer thinkin'! Not with me 'ands, yer soppy ha'porth! Kinda sortin' 'em over ter find out which I like best.'

'Be careful you don't come to harm,' I told her.

'Yo sound like me mum' she replied, smiling.

After Lizzie and I had wished each other good night, I watched her run for the tram. I wouldn't see her again until Monday morning when we clocked in. Once I asked her where she lived, but all she said was in a back street in Smethwick and that one day she would take me to meet her mum, sisters and brothers. She never mentioned her dad, and when I asked about him she said, 'Don't be too nosy, I'll tell yer one day, or me mum will.'

As I turned the corner I saw Frankie again. 'What are you doing here?' I asked.

'I've bin waitin' ter tell yer the news. I told yer I was goin' ter do a bit o' snoopin'. Well, we've got Liza this time!' Frankie always tried to sound dramatic when explaining something.

'Let's go in the fish shop out of the cold,' I suggested.

'Yes, we'll 'ave a plate of chips while I tell yer,' he agreed.

As we began to eat our vinegared chips, he looked pleased with himself and went about telling me what he had discovered. 'I waited till Mum and Liza had gone ter the market, then I begun ter look in some likely places where she 'ides 'er things. The last place I looked was the attic. When I looked under the bed, I found 'er tin box and looked inside and saw there was only 'er jack stones, some coloured beads, a pen and some bits of chalk.' He nearly choked on a chip as he began to say, 'When I looked in the bed an' dad's old Army coat fell on the floor, I 'eard something rattle, an' when I felt in the pocket, what der yer think I found? Guess. No, three guesses,' he cried out excitedly.

'I can't! So hurry up and spit it out!'

'Yer know yer mum sometimes gets Liza ter write a letter ter Jack, when yer not 'ere and she puts a silver sixpence inside a packet o' Woodbines. Well, when I felt inside the pocket I couldn't believe what I found – a Woodbine packet, two whole cigarettes, three nubs, tuppence an' . . .'

'No! Yer can't mean to say she never posted them?'

'How else wud 'er get 'em!'

'Maybe they're Dad's,' I suggested.

'Don't be daft, Katie. Dad only smokes a pipe, and I've found a letter too. So do yer want ter come in an' 'ear the verdict?'

'I can't wait to hear her lie her way out of this one,' I replied.

❖

We entered the room and found Mum sitting by the fire with her feet resting on the sofa. Liza was sitting on the sofa sucking a sweet.

'Yo two took yer time comin 'ome! Now yer can put the kettle on, Katie, and mek me a cuppa tea.'

Frankie pointed to Liza. 'What's 'er doin' as she can't mek it?'

'She's bin ter the market with me! Don't yer come 'ere givin' yer orders out! Katie'll do what I say. Now put that kettle on an' let's 'ave less of yer bloody old buck!'

I often wished I could have stood up to my mother the way my brother did, but I was afraid of the consequences. I was now becoming more nervous than before. I wouldn't put it past her to throw something at us, so I decided to put the kettle on. As I went to it, Frankie cried, 'Don't yer dare, Katie! Not until Mum 'ears what I gotta say!'

Mum glared at us and shouted, 'I'd like ter know what's gooin' on between the pair of yer!'

'This is nothing ter do with Kate, Mum, it's that little thief, lookin' all innocent with that smug look on 'er face!'

'What yer mean a thief?' Mum exclaimed.

'Ask 'er where 'er got 'er cigarettes from when I saw the three of 'em smoking in the brewhouse!'

'He's lyin', Mum!' Liza flared up. 'I ain't bin near the brewhouse. Nor smokin'. He's makin' it all up!'

'Now, Liza, yo just be quiet while I 'ear what 'e's gotta say.'

Before Frankie could say another word Liza gave herself away. 'It warn't me, Mum. It was George and little Freddie Freer!'

'Who's George?'

'Her name's Georgina,' Frankie interrupted, 'that bossy boss-eyed girl 'er goes about with.'

'What do yer know about this, Kate?' Mum asked.

'I don't know anything,' I replied. 'Only what Frankie has told me.'

'Now, Frankie,' Mum said more calmly. 'Let's 'ave the 'ole story.'

Frankie told her how he found the cigarette packet with the cigarettes and the coppers, also the letter Liza was supposed to have posted. Mum suddenly jumped up from the chair, almost knocking the stool in the fire, and, grabbing hold of Liza, she slapped her face several times. 'Come on now!' Mum yelled. 'I want the bloody truth or else!'

'I meant ter post it, Mum, really I did, but I fergot,' Liza whined.

'Yer not only a thief, yer a bloody liar too!'

I could see that Mum was really going to punish her, so I made my way out of the house in case she started throwing things. As soon as I got as far as the corner I saw Frankie. 'I don't know what's goin' ter 'appen when Dad finds out,' he said as he came up to me.

'I bet she won't tell him,' I replied.

'She says she will, and Liza is goin' ter tell what Mum's done ter 'er!'

'What's she done now?'

'Well, she laid 'er on the table an' pulled down 'er drawers and started ter beat 'er with Dad's strap. When I tried ter stop 'er, she landed one on me, so I ran out!'

'We'd better go back before she does more damage to her.'

'All right, Kate, if yer think it will 'elp. But yer know Mum when 'er finds out any of us lyin', Frankie said.

'But Frankie, it's theft of the cigarettes and her smoking that's made it worse, I wish you hadn't told.'

'Why? An' let 'er get away with it? I'm glad in one way, it's about time Mum found out what she's really like.'

We hesitated for a while, making our minds up whether to interfere, but Frankie said it would be best to go in now before matters got worse. We stood listening outside the door and were surprised to find it so quiet.

'I wonder what's happened?' I whispered.

'I don't like it, we better go in an' see,' he replied.

Frankie peered round the door. 'Mum and Liza ain't 'ere. I wonder what's 'appened now! Mum could 'ave killed 'er the mood she's in!'

'Oh, God! Don't say that, Frankie!'

'I'll go and look in Mum's bedroom,' he replied. 'You go up ter the attic.'

But I was too scared to move, thinking what I might find. As soon as I managed to put one foot on the first step of the stairs I called out, 'Liza, are you up there?' No answer. I called out, 'Liza, are you all right? It's me, Katie.' Still no answer. I was beginning to get morbid thoughts just as Frankie touched my shoulder; I nearly fell down the stairs with fright.

'I called out but there's no answer an' I ain't going up there by myself.'

'I'll goo if yer scared, but Mum ain't in, 'er shawl's missing.' He soon came down to say Liza wasn't there.

'Perhaps she's down the cellar.'

'Don't be so bloody morbid an' stop shakin'. I'll go down if it'll satisfy yer.' I dreaded to hear what he would find, but when he came back he said there was no one down there, only the rats. 'An' they're not as scared as you are,' he reported. 'Per'aps Mum's took 'er ter the police station.'

We were about to ask some of our neighbours when we saw Mum coming down the yard. She went inside the house and we followed her in, 'Shut that bloody dower!' she shouted. 'I don't want the nosy neighbours listenin'. 'Ave yer seen anythin' of Liza?' she asked more calmly.

'No, Mum,' Frankie replied. 'What's happened ter her?'

'I don't know. After I give 'er a couple o' beatings with yer dad's strap, I 'ad ter let 'er goo an' now she's run away and God knows where to. I know I ought never ter 'ave used that strap on 'er, but it was the fust time and I swear I'll never use it agen!'

'She won't go far,' Frankie reassured her. 'She'll soon be back.'

'Can yer think of any place where she could goo?'

'I know,' I piped up. 'I think she's gone to tell that wench she calls George.'

'Do yer know where she lives?' he asked.

'She lives in Aston with her stepmother and that man she calls Herbut. You remember, where Grandma used to visit before she died.'

'What street's that?' Mum asked.

'Moland Street in Aston,' I said. (Now the site of Aston University.)

'Well, yo 'ad better goo and find 'er an' bring 'er back afower yer dad gets 'ome.'

We didn't need telling twice, and she didn't even give us the pennies for the trolley bus. As soon as we turned the corner to Moland Street, I showed my brother where the house was. It was up the second entry on the right, and as we walked up and across the yard, I pointed out the house. It stood in the corner away from many more back-to-back derelict houses.

'Good God, it's worst than our dump!' Frankie commented.

There were cats and mongrel dogs running around the yard and little naked children playing in the gutter. After stepping over urine and faeces we eventually got to number nineteen.

The door was opened by a tall, hefty feller who yelled, 'Sod off, the pair o' yer, afower I puts me boot up yer arses! Comin' 'ere beggin'.'

'We ain't come beggin',' Frankie answered. 'We've come ter see if our sister's 'ere.'

'We ain't got no bloody sister 'ere!'

'Well, is your daughter in?' I asked nervously.

'Which one yer want? There's four of 'em and they ain't mine!'

'Her name's Georgina,' Frankie replied.

'My sister always comes to your place with Georgina,' I managed to say.

'What's yer sister's name then?' he asked.

'Liza, Liza Greenhill.'

'Well, why dain't yer say in the fust place? She's gone with George ter the fruit shop.'

Before we could thank him, he slammed the door in our faces.

As we managed to walk down that slimy cobbled yard, we noticed several neighbours come out and stare at us, then as we turned the corner back into Aston Street we saw Liza and Georgina, arm in arm, eating a toffee apple on a stick. When Liza saw us she cried out, 'What are you doin' 'ere? If yer think I'm comin' home with the two of yer, yer got another think comin'. I'm stayin' with Georgie's mum and Herbut!'

'Who said so?' asked Georgina suddenly.

'Herbut said. He likes me an' I can stay as long as I like.'

'Liar, liar! Herbut don't like yer, nor me mum! They said so.'

'Yer only jealous 'cos Herbut makes a fuss of me and he . . .'

'Come on, Liza,' Frankie exclaimed. 'We don't want ter 'ear any more. I think we've 'eard enough. Now yer coming home with us or do we 'ave ter tell Mum and let 'er fetch yer or what?'

'Come on, Liza,' I said. 'Don't make things worse for yerself, yer can see Georgina don't want yer to stay.'

'Yer can come agen when yer want, but I'll 'ave ter go now before 'Erbut comes lookin' fer me.'

As Georgina ran round the corner, Liza began to weep. I noticed she wasn't pretending this time. 'But Katie, I don't want ter go back ter the house fer Mum ter beat me agen with that strap!' she exclaimed.

'You'll be surprised to know she said she was sorry and that she would never use the strap again. Wipe yer eyes and finish eatin' yer toffee apple.'

'I don't want any more,' she sniffed.

'Well, give it 'ere, I'll finish it,' said Frankie.

As she handed the toffee apple to him she said, 'I wish I'd posted Jack's letter, but it was George who tempted me to keep the sixpence and the Woodbines.'

'Let that be a lesson in future, not to lie or steal,' I said, 'because you'll always be found out.'

'You've lied, Katie!'

'Yes, but never stole, and I've only told little white lies. Anyway, I'll be sending Mum's letters to Jack in future.'

'Come on, you two,' Frankie urged. 'We've a long way ter go and I've got me paper round ter do.'

When we got home, Frankie left us, and Liza and I went on into the house. I couldn't believe my eyes for as soon as Mum saw us she leapt from her chair and threw her arms around Liza. 'I'm sorry I beat yer, Liza, but I'll never use that strap agen.'

'Are yer goin' ter tell me dad?' Liza asked.

'No, luv. I wun't tell 'im this time.'

'Nor what I dun?' Liza asked.

'No, luv. Any'ow, Katie's gooin' ter write an' post me letters ter Jack in future.'

I felt quite disgusted with them both; I knew Liza was Mum's favourite but I never expected this. At least Mum could have given her a lecture. I don't believe they heard me leave, but I knew one thing: I held that secret against my mother and the strap, and if she ever beat me again I would tell.

A few days later I was upstairs cleaning out the attic, when I heard my mum and dad quarrelling.

'It's yer own fault, yer've always let that one 'ave her own way! Whatever happens in the future, don't yer ever let me hear of yer using that strap on her agen or you'll answer ter me!'

'But, Sam, I dain't realise what I was doin'. I only 'it her twice.'

'I don't understand you at times, Polly. If only you'd have let me teach yer how to read and write you'd have a better outlook on life.'

'Oh, don't bring that up agen!'

'Very well. But remember, you can punish her, but not with that strap!'

'But 'ow did yo know about it? I suppose Katie told yer!'

'Katie hasn't told me anything. Anyway, she never carries tales.'

'Was it Frankie?'

'No. It was one of the neighbours who heard her screams.'

'But why carn't yer tek 'er in 'and? She's gettin' worse since 'er's bin mixin' with that George.'

'Polly, I've tried to teach her to tell the truth and God knows I'm losing my patience! But you spoil her by giving way to her and believing all the lies she tells yer.'

'What about the others?' Mum exclaimed. 'Yer've never seen any wrong in them!'

'No. Because I know when they tell the truth! But I've gone past chastising that little lying varmint, and if you don't take her in hand there's only one place she'll end up, and that's the House of Correction!'

'Don't yer dare remind me o' thet place! It wasn't all my fault I was sent there.' I heard her begin to cry.

As I came downstairs I saw Dad put his arms around her. 'I'm sorry, Polly. I didn't wish to remind yer. Now put yer shawl on and I'll take yer out for a walk and a drink.'

As she wiped her eyes and draped her shawl round her shoulders, she said, 'I know she'll change, Sam, when 'er's older.'

'We'll have ter wait and see,' Dad said. 'Now forget about Liza, but if you do have any more trouble with her, I want ter know about it. We won't be long, Katie,' he called out. 'Just keep a good fire and kettle boiling for when we get back.'

When leaving work on Saturday afternoons, Lizzie and I would promise to meet later to queue up at the Royal Picture Palace, also known as the Monkey Run, in Soho Road.

After giving Mum my keep money, I would put some away to buy myself better clothes. Mum never seemed to bother me now that I was earning, but it was always the usual warning when I got ready to go out. 'Yo be careful wot yo get up to! An' come straight back 'ome!'

'I'm only going to the pictures with Lizzie,' I told her.

'An' another thing. That wench yer meetin' is older than yo', so I'm warnin' yer if yer get in any trouble.'

'What difference does her age make? I like her and she's fun to be with.'

'Well, yo be careful, yer know what'll 'appen if

yer bring any trouble 'ome!' she warned.

'Yes, Mum, I've heard it so many times I'm not likely to forget.'

'Well, just yo remember.' She pointed her finger at me.

I wanted to say, 'Isn't it about time you checked up on Liza with that Buckley lad next door', but I knew it would have caused another argument, and would be a waste of time anyway. I was in a hurry to get out of the house and meet my friend.

Lizzie was already waiting for me in the queue, where I saw her flirting with a couple of fellers, but when they gave me the glad eye, I ignored them. I didn't know that she already knew them.

As we paid our threepence I was glad to hear the usherette say, 'Single seats only.' When Lizzie whispered, 'Just our luck', I whispered back, 'I don't mind.' I didn't realise that it was planned we should all sit together. When the picture was over and we got outside, there was no sign of them. It was obvious Lizzie was expecting them to be there. As we called for our usual drink of sarsaparilla at the little herb shop, I saw Lizzie looking for them, but they were not among the customers. By the time we had finished it was ten o'clock and I had to go home. I wished Lizzie good night and said I would see her on Monday morning, and we parted.

On the way home I felt someone tap on my shoulder and when I looked round it was one of those two fellers I had seen in the queue.

'Hello, Katie. All alone?' he asked.

'What's it ter do with you? Anyway, how do *you* know my name?'

'Lizzie told me. Can I walk you home?'

He seemed a nice enough chap, but I never did trust the opposite sex.

'No, yer carn't!' I snapped. 'My brother is coming to meet me,' I lied, 'so you had better go before he comes.'

'I'm sorry if I have offended you, but I was going to ask if you would come to a show with me sometime. I would like your company and you can trust me to bring you home safely. My name's Gregory Bibbs. I live with my mum and dad and four sisters in Albion Street.'

I was about to say, 'that's not far from where I live', but thought it was better not to tell him. While we had been talking, time was going by and I had to be indoors by just gone ten at the latest.

'I'm sorry but I never go out alone, only sometimes with my brother Frankie or my friend Lizzie.'

'How long have you known her?'

'A few weeks. We work together. Why?'

'Now, don't get me wrong, but let me give you a bit of advice. Lizzie Farrell is not the sort of girl to be seen out with.'

'And why not?' I exclaimed angrily. 'What's it to do with you whom I go out with?'

'She's courting my brother Tom and flirtin' with every chap that takes her fancy. One of these days she's going to get herself in trouble!'

'I don't believe yer!' I replied as I hurried away.

'Well, if you want the truth, ask her yourself,' he called out after me.

As soon as I got indoors, Mum was waiting for me.

'What bloody time yer call this?' she cried out, pointing to the alarm clock on the shelf. 'It's a quarter ter eleven. Where yer bin till now?'

I dared not tell her the truth so I told her we stopped to have a drink in the herb shop.

'Well, that don't tek yer till now ter get 'ome. That Lizzie is gooin' ter get the length of me tongue when 'er calls fer yer agen.'

'It's not her fault.'

'I want yer indoors at ten o'clock in future or yer don't see that Lizzie Farrell any mower. Now get yer supper and then yo can fetch Liza from next dower afower yer dad gets in.'

'But why can't Frankie fetch her?'

'Frankie's out courtin'. At least I don't 'ave ter worry over 'im,' she told me.

'But why not?' I replied.

''Cos 'e's a lad, ain't 'e! Lads can look after 'emselves. It's only wenches that mothers 'ave ter worry about!'

Although Mum never explained properly, I knew what she meant.

Learning Life's Lessons

I was always happiest when Monday morning came to get me out of the house and with my friend at the factory. Often Lizzie made me laugh at her comical sayings and the things she talked about. But talking or smoking during working hours was a fine, dismissal or both. The only time workers could talk was during the ten-minute break at mid-morning, when all machines stopped. The next break was our dinner time, one till two. Many had their break eating their sandwiches as they sat at their machines, but Lizzie and I would hurry to clock out so that we could have our dinner and a good chat at a small cook shop in Snow Hill, before the crowd got there.

The cook shop had once been a large dwelling house and was now owned by a woman and her crippled sister; both of their husbands were away in France. They did all their own cooking on the premises, and although the windows were often steamed up, you could almost taste that mouth-watering aroma across the street. Often Lizzie and I would pool our few coppers. Sometimes we had two faggots with mushy peas and mashed potatoes for sixpence. Other days it was two sausages, two eggs and chips, or rabbit pie and vegetables with thick brown gravy and a chunk of bread. On Saturday we would have a real blow-out with hip-bone steak and three veg for tenpence and a mug of tea for one penny. For afters we would sometimes have a piece of baked custard, rice pudding, spotted dick, jam roly-poly, or bread pudding for twopence. There was none of your frozen factory food packets. It was all good wholesome fare. Those were the days.

Although I didn't entirely believe what Gregory Bibbs had told me about Lizzie, I began to have my doubts about her. Sometimes, after promising to meet me at the tram stop, she would either turn up too late for the pictures or wouldn't turn up at all. When I asked why, she would say her mother was ill and she had to stay at home to look after younger brothers and sisters. I believed her, until one night I was getting ready to meet her outside the Regal Picture House when my brother walked in. As soon as he asked me where I was going and I told him, he said, 'Kate, don't yer think yer should give 'er the cold shoulder. She'll only let yer down again.'

'It's not her fault, Frankie. Her mother's been ill and she sometimes has to stay and look after her.'

'That's what she tells you, Kate, but I've seen her mum

several times when she's let yer down and she didn't look ill ter me!'

'I don't believe yer!' I replied angrily.

'Very well. If yer don't believe me, ask Nellie. We both saw 'er arm in arm with two fellers I know, going into the Frightened Horse pub. And another thing, Kate, Mum's got ter hear yer've been seen along the Monkey Run with 'er and two chaps an' now . . .'

'That's a lie! I always come straight home by myself when I leave Lizzie at the tram stop.'

'I believe yer, Kate. But will Mum? If yer want ter avoid any trouble, you tell Lizzie what I have just told you, and if she denies it then it's up ter you ter give her up.'

'But she's the only friend I've got, Frankie. I don't see any wrong in her. Anyway, what am I to do? Stay indoors on Saturday night?'

'Yer always welcome ter come ter the pictures with Nellie and me, you know that.'

'No, thanks,' I replied. 'I don't want to be a gooseberry.'

'Well, please yerself, Katie, but the offer's still there if yer change yer mind. Any'ow yer wouldn't find it diffi-cult ter get a nice boyfriend. There's a nice chap only twelve months older than you works with me, who lives with his widowed mother. He's often told me he'd like ter tek yer out.'

'I'll find my own friend if I need one!' I snapped.

'Well, what yer goin' ter do now?' Frankie asked.

'I think I'll stay indoors tonight and put some records on the old gramophone and finish that scarf I'm knitting for your birthday,' I told him.

When he had gone, I sat down by the fire and began to think about what he had told me. I knew Frankie would never lie to me, and after what he had said I had to find out Lizzie's version. Should I put my coat and hat on and go out and see if she was waiting for me? No, I said to myself, it will be better to wait until Monday and hear what she has to say when I confront her.

Just as I got out my knitting and was putting on the old cracked record, in walked Liza with another of her young chaps. Surprised to see me sitting there, she asked, 'What are yo doin' 'ere? I thought it was yer night out with Lizzie Farrell?'

'No, I've changed my mind. I'm staying in for a change.'

'But yer carn't!' said Liza.

'And why can't I?'

'Because me an' Dave want ter talk about summat private.'

'Does Mum know?'

'No! An' yo know what ter expect if yer tell 'er!' Liza snapped.

'Mum will find out herself and when she does there'll be sparks flying.'

'Come on, Dave. She's only jealous 'cos she ain't got a fella ter tek 'er out.'

I just shrugged my shoulders as they went out. Wherever they were going to do their courting, I didn't care.

Left alone with my thoughts, I got some frocks and undergarments that needed mending. After finishing them and some other odd jobs, I was beginning to feel tired. It was time to go to bed before Mum came home asking questions. As I lay there, I kept wondering what I was going to say to Lizzie on Monday morning. It was at such times as these that I needed a mother's under-standing, someone to confide in and to teach me the facts of life. I don't think my mum knew what was expected of her.

I was still feeling upset and angry when I walked into the machine shop on Monday morning ready to face Lizzie. The machinery started and I knew the punishment if the notices on the wall were ignored, therefore I had to wait until the ten-minute break for our snack and a cup of tea. As soon as the hooter went for break she came over to me full of apology.

'I'm sorry, Kate. I dain't turn up ter meet yer, me . . .'

'Don't bother with your excuses, I didn't intend to turn up myself after I found out the lies you've told me!' I exclaimed. 'I suppose you were going ter tell me about your mum being ill?'

'She is ill, I told yer! That's why I couldn't keep me promise!'

'You're a liar!' I shouted for all to hear. 'You were seen arm in arm with two fellers when you'd promised to see me.'

'Who's told yer that?'

'My brother and his girlfriend, Nellie! Save yer lies for somebody else, I don't want anything more ter do with you, so if . . .' I told her.

'Keep yer voice down,' she whispered.

'I don't care who's listening. Deny it if you can.' I

replied angrily. Just as she was about to answer, the hooter sounded for us to begin work.

As soon as it was one o'clock she came over again, and tried to tell me something but I said I didn't want to hear.

'But, Kate,' I heard her say, 'there's a lot I 'ave ter tell yer, but I don't know 'ow ter begin.'

'More lies?'

'No, Kate! But I carn't tell yer 'ere.'

'I don't want to know,' I replied.

'Please will yer meet me when we finish work and I'll try an' explain why I've let yer down. I want ter tell yer the truth, believe me, Katie.'

But I was adamant, I wasn't even interested. 'No! I don't want to hear nor go out with you ever agen! My mum would kill me if she found out.'

'Well, I'll ter yer one thing! Yer won't see me agen after Thursday.'

We never spoke during the next two days and on Friday she didn't come in, nor Saturday to draw her wages. I began to wonder why and wished I had listened to what she had to tell me.

After collecting my wage packet, I made my way out into the street where I saw a grey-haired woman staring up at the brass sign over the office door. She wore a man's grey cap on the back of her head, a ragged grey shawl around her shoulders and a long black frock. On her feet were a pair of well-worn men's boots. She seemed to be waiting for someone. When I asked, she replied, 'Can yer tell me if this is where me daughter werked?'

'What's her name?'

'Elizabeth Farrell. I'm 'er mother. I've come fer 'er wages. Will yer show me the way in?'

'Is Lizzie ill?'

'No! She ain't.'

'I'm Lizzie's friend, Katie.'

'Katie who?'

'Katie Greenhill. We worked together, side by side.'

'She dain't mention no Katie Greenhill ter me!'

'But she must have! We used to meet some Saturday nights and go ter the pictures together.'

'That's new ter me. That bleedin' lyin' little varmint told me she spent 'er Saturday nights with 'er aunt 'an cousins in West Brom. Any'ow, she wunt be comin' back ter work fer sumtime now.'

'Can I have your address and come and see her, Mrs Farrell?' I asked.

'No, yer carn't!' she snapped.

'But why? What's she done?'

'Never yo mind. She's gooin' away an' she wunt be back fer a long time. But if she's got yower address I carn't stop 'er writin' to yer. Now will yer please show me where ter goo?'

As I knocked on the office door I heard the fore-woman's voice call, 'Come in.' Mrs Powell was sitting behind her desk sorting papers. As we entered I became very nervous. Before she could say a word, I said, 'Madam, this is Lizzie's mother, Mrs Farrell.'

Lizzie's mother was busy looking at the office.

'Mrs Farrell,' I said, nudging her, 'tell her what you've come for.'

'I've come fer me daughter's pay, 'an 'er insurance cards.'

'How do I know you're her mother?' asked Mrs Powell.

'I've brought a note from 'er an' 'er birth certificate.'

'Why does she want to leave?'

'I'm ashamed ter tell yer,' came Mrs Farrell's reply.

'Well, you'll have to, before I can hand over what you're asking for,' Mrs Powell told her.

I saw Mrs Farrell lean over the desk and I tried to listen to her whispering but all I heard was, 'An' that's the truth as God is me judge.'

'Very well,' the forewoman replied, 'but I was expecting her to call herself. After what you have told me I would have sacked her anyway. Now wait here while I get her insurance cards and wage packet.'

After handing them over, she was still frowning as she pushed a document towards Mrs Farrell. 'Sign here!' she snapped. But Mrs Farrell's signature was just an 'X'.

'I don't think that will do,' Mrs Powell said.

'But I carn't write.'

'Very well. Greenhill, you had better sign it below as a witness, then you can both leave.'

As soon as we got into the street, I asked again if I could go and see Lizzie, but she still refused. As I began to walk away, she called me back. 'If yo'll tek my advice, luv, yo'll ferget 'er. It ain't the fust time 'er's brought on us this kind of trouble.'

'Why won't yer tell me? P'raps I can help?'

Her eyes filled with tears. 'Yer carnt 'elp 'er this time. Now yo goo 'ome, luv, an' ferget about 'er.'

As she left me standing there I wondered what sort of trouble Lizzie had got herself into. It must be something serious. Had she been stealing and in prison, or was she in the family way?

For a long time I couldn't get Lizzie off my mind. Each day I began to miss her more and more. Why hadn't I listened to her when she tried to tell me her trouble? Little did I know that many months later I would meet up with her.

I didn't stay long at the Brass Works. A few days later I found work at Lucus's in Great King Street where I began work on a power press. The job was hard and very dirty on my hands, face and clothes. Mum was always nagging about not getting the oil out, but the wages were good and I was able to dress myself more in the fashion of the day. Although there were several young fellers I worked with wanting to date me, I always refused them. I was also hoping that some day I would meet up with Lizzie again. It wasn't that I didn't like the opposite sex, but each time I was asked for a date my mum's warnings came to remind me: 'Don't let a feller kiss yer or the next thing yer'll be 'avin' a babby, an' that means the work'ouse or put in an 'ome.'

I never kept a job of work for more than a few months, always wanting a change. The men, women and even young girls at Lucus's, swore like troopers when things went wrong. I heard enough bad language at home and amongst our neighbours, but this was not easy for me, I was shy and nervous and so it was difficult for me to make friends.

Each night I would glance at the ads to find something better than working on an oily power press. One Thursday evening I came home from work and picked up Dad's newspaper off the step outside, but before I could look at it, Dad called, 'Is that my *Mail*, Katie?' I gave him the paper and listened to him reading out the headlines to my mother. I knew I had to wait until he had finished and then I would cut up a page to make spills for his clay pipe. These were always placed in a crock jam jar in the steel fender beside the fire place. I had to cut the other pages into squares to hang on the inside of the door to our communal closet. (The print never came off on your bottom as it would today!)

One night I spread the last page on the living-room table, and when doing this I noticed an advert saying, 'Good prospects for girls 16–18 years'. I didn't stop to read it all, but tore it out before Mum saw me and slipped it down my bloomers.

I lit the candle with a spill and went down the yard to hang the paper squares on the closet door. I pulled down my bloomers, sat on the wooden seat and began to read: 'Young girls wanted 16–18 with good singing voice. Good prospects. Apply between 12 and 1 Saturday. 164 Corporation Street.'

Hiding the piece of paper back in my bloomers, I went inside and washed my hands.

After supper, having done some more chores, I took myself off to bed. I knew I could sing well, my teacher had often told me that all I needed was some training, but it was more than I dare ask my parents for and they couldn't afford the money anyway.

I went to work the next morning but I couldn't concentrate. I knew I couldn't apply on my own; I had to confide in someone and ask advice.

That same evening when I was washing my hands to go home, one of the girls who worked in the office asked if I was worried about something. 'Why do you ask?'

'You wasn't concentrating on your job and you might have had an accident. Would you like to tell me what the trouble is and maybe I can help?'

'Yes!' I exclaimed. 'Look at my hands! Cut and bleeding and my nails all broken!'

'I'm sorry, Katie. There's nothing I can do unless you want to leave and find another job.'

'I've tried, Ellen, but I don't make friends very easily. I'd like to go out and enjoy the company of young lads with the girls I work with, but it's more than I dare to defy my mum, so now I've decided to answer this advert and see if I can better myself, but I think I'm too shy to go about it.'

'Will you let me see, perhaps I can help?' As soon as she read it she asked, 'Would you like me to come with you?'

'Yes please, Ellen,' I replied eagerly. 'Will you?'

'Saturday morning, the firm's closing for stocktaking and my mum and dad are away for the weekend, so if you'd like to come home with me I'll see what I can do for your figure!' she told me.

'But what's me figure got ter do with me voice?'

'Well, you often speak nicely, Katie, and you're also attractive. They'll notice these things as well as your singing voice.'

'What's the matter with me figure?'

'Well, for one thing, you're too plump around the waist, you've got small titties and . . .'

'What's the matter with me titties? I can't do anything about them!' I exclaimed.

'I can try if you'll let me, but first you'll have to come home with me tomorrow morning and I'll see what I can do. Can you meet me at 8 o'clock outside the George and Dragon? And no more ifs an' buts,' she added.

'Yes,' I replied as I walked away, 'I'll remember.'

Saturday morning, Dad had lit the fire early before leaving for work. I took Mum's usual cup of tea up to her in bed, then went to get ready. I put on my best Sunday frock and shoes and was ready to go out when I heard Mum call down the stairs. 'Kate, bring me up a piece of toast!'

I made believe I hadn't heard her as I quietly closed the door behind me.

Ellen Handley only lived about ten minutes' walk away, the house was built in the same way as ours, but it was not untidy and cluttered up as ours was. As she was making a pot of tea, she told me she was nearly eighteen, that her dad had been twice married, that she loved her stepmother, and soon they were going to live in Canada. I told her about the rest of my family, and when we had finished our cup of tea she said it was time to get undressed and ready for the interview. I only slipped off my frock, and as I stood there waiting she said, 'Don't be shy of me, you'll have to take them nearly all off if you want me to get you ready. Anyway, I only want you to try on a pair of corsets, to give you a better figure, the only thing is I've lost the suspenders.'

'I don't think that'll matter, I roll me stockings past me knees anyway,' I told her.

'If you're too shy to undress, I'll go in the kitchen and leave you to try them on.

As I stripped down to my calico chemise and liberty bodice and tried the corsets on, Ellen came in to lighten the laces. She told me to look in the mirror and what a difference those corsets made to my figure!

'Now,' she said, 'we've got to do something about those little titties of yours.'

'But why?' I asked. 'What's wrong with them?'

'Well, they're not like mine are they, Katie, as you can see?'

I felt embarrassed and tried to look away when she opened her blouse and showed me her full, rounded breasts. I couldn't believe they were so large, and when I asked if she had milk in them she smiled, 'Don't be daft, Katie! You only have milk when you're having a baby. Now, stand still while I stuff some cotton wool down there.'

'But what if it falls out when I start walking?' I asked.

'I'm going to stick them down with a couple of plasters,' she said,

After Ellen had performed on me, she told me to look in the mirror again. I was surprised and pleased to see the change it had made.

After I got dressed, with a dab of Phul-Nana face powder and lipstick we were soon on our way to Jeromes in Bull Street to have my hair cut and marcel-waved, and then to have my photograph taken. It was now ten past twelve and I was ready for the interview. We arrived outside the derelict building. 'This can't be the place, Ellen!'

'Well, it does say 164.'

'But there's no name, only a placard: "Inquire on the second floor".'

When I asked Ellen to come with me, she replied, 'It's you they'll want to see, not me. Now you've got this far so don't be nervous. I'll wait for you in that little coffee shop across the street. I'll keep me fingers crossed, so off you go and good luck!' She pecked my cheek and I watched her go.

As I pushed open the well-weathered oak door, I noticed that inside it was dark and dusty and there were eighteen uneven stairs to climb to the first narrow landing, where there was a flicker of light coming from a gas jet inside a wire cage on the wall. After counting the next fifteen stairs, I came to a green painted door with a notice on it: 'Please knock before entering'. When I knocked I heard a man's voice, 'See who that is, Olga.'

The woman opened the door and gazed at me. She was made up with red painted cheeks and lipstick. She looked about fifty, wore a bright purple gown and had a mop of red hair which could have been a wig. But what stood out most was her large bosom, which made her look like a pouter pigeon. 'Well!' she cried out abruptly. 'What's your business?'

'I've come for an interview,' I replied nervously.

'And which one's that?'

'It's the advert I read about you wanting a singer.'

'Very well, yer better go in.'

She almost pushed me inside that stuffy room, and as she went out and closed the door behind her I saw a bald-headed man with broad shoulders. I couldn't see what he looked like because he had his face buried in a racing paper, sitting at his desk with his back towards me. As I waited for him to turn round and ask me questions, I glanced around the room. On his desk were strewn several papers, a writing pad, a pen, a jar of ink and a very full ashtray. Beside the telephone was a half bottle of whisky. On the other side of the room was a red plush couch, two chairs and worn lino on the floor, and around the walls were photographs of film stars and actors, Mary Pickford, Nellie Wallace, Mae West, Florrie Ford, Gertie Gertarna, Hetty King, Harold Lloyd, Buster Keaton, Fatty Arbuckle, and many, many more. By this time I was feeling disappointed. I had hoped to be interviewed in a nice comfortable office and not to be ignored.

Thinking he had forgotten I was there, I scraped back the chair I had sat down on and gave a loud cough. As he put his paper on the desk and turned to face me, I could see he wore thick pebble glasses, and when he stared across at me I thought he looked like an owl with a bulbous nose. I didn't know whether to walk out or stay. When he began to ask my name and age, his voice sounded very pleasant to the ear. Each time he asked me a question he called me love, my dear and darling, words I'd never been used to hearing and I felt flattered.

He asked me what I wanted to be.

'A singer, sir.'

'Very well, my dear. Let me hear you sing a few notes, darling.'

I began with 'On the Banks of Alan Water', but once I started I didn't want to stop. After a couple of lines he interrupted, 'Yes! Yes! That will be enough for now, darling. You have a sweet voice and you're a very pretty girl too. Have your parents helped you to sing, dear, I mean . . .'

'No, sir. Me mum don't like me singing around the house and she never lets me make up, but you see I . . .'

'Very well, love. Just stand over by the window where I can get a better look at you.'

As he came over towards me, I noticed his arms and legs were short for his body. I began to feel sorry for him, for I was used to seeing deformed people in and around the district where I lived, but when he came closer to me and asked me to lift my frock up, I shook my head from side to side.

'Don't be shy, darling. I'll not only want you to sing but dance too. That's why I want to see the shape of your legs.'

'But I can't dance! I've never been taught, apart from a knees-up when we have a party in our back yard, or when the barrel organ man comes,' I managed to blurt out.

I didn't like the way he laughed at me, but when I felt his podgy hands trying to squeeze my cotton-wool titties, I knew at once what his intentions were! Suddenly, with all the force I could find, I brought my knee up and caught him in the 'John Willie'. He fell across the couch, moaning and swearing as to what he was going to do to me.

I fled through the door and down those two flights of stairs as if the devil himself was after me. I never stopped running until I reached the little coffee shop where Ellen was waiting for me.

'You've been a long while,' she said. 'Are you all right?'

'Oh, Ellen. That dirty old ram across the road tried to have me, but when he tried to squeeze . . .'

'Don't shout so loud, everyone's staring at us!'

'I don't care who stares, or hears, I'm going to tell the police!'

'All right, Katie. Calm down and let's get out of here. You can tell me on the way home.'

As we walked down towards Snow Hill, I began to tell her what had happened. 'He didn't want a singer, all he wanted was my body! I had ter knee him before he'd let go of me. If you'd have come with me when I asked yer to, it wouldn't have happened!' Tears ran down my cheeks.

'Don't blame me! It was you who wanted the job, not me. Believe me, Katie, I wouldn't have let you go in there if I had known.'

'I'm sorry I snapped at you, Ellen, but I was so scared.'

'Never mind, dry your eyes and put it down to experience.'

When we got to her house, there was still a good fire burning, the kettle was singing on the hob and we cut some potted meat sandwiches. As we sat beside the fire eating and drinking a cup of tea, she began to talk. 'What I'm going to tell you will help you to learn from my mistakes and be on your guard against plausible men. I was an only child spoilt by my parents and my aunt Matilda, who took me wherever they went on holiday. I was nearly fifteen when they moved from West Bromwich and bought a detached house in a nice district of Dudley, a few doors from my aunt. On my fifteenth birthday, Mum told me she was going to have a baby, a brother or sister for me to love. Aunt Matilda and I spent many hours making baby clothes, and helping Mum during her pregnancy. But four months later she had a bad haemorrhage, and four days after that she died. It was a sad loss for us, and after the funeral, I don't think Dad could ever get over what had happened. He began neglecting me and the home and staying out late at night, drinking.

Aunty warned him about leaving me alone at night to fend for myself and threatened to take me away to live with her. After that warning he began to be his old self again, but often when he sat alone I would see him gazing into the fire. I knew his thoughts were with my mum. When I told Aunty that he was often moody, she would reply, 'I know, it's a sad loss to lose someone we love, but we can't live with the dead. Life must go on and perhaps some day he will find someone to spend his life with again.'

'A few months later I met him arm in arm with a woman in the park. When we were introduced, he told me he was going to marry her and that she would be company for me while he was away on business.'

'What did you say, Ellen? What was she like?' I asked.

'It was his affair. She was dressed smart and was very good looking, and I think about the same age as my father. After a while I began to like her and she liked me too.'

'Better than the mother you lost?'

'Well, yes, Katie. My mother often quarrelled with me and would say my dad thought more of me than he did of her. When I told my aunty she said all women say things like that when they are pregnant. But I knew she was a bit jealous of me at times. Anyway, three weeks later my dad and Maud were married and went on holiday abroad for a month.'

'Did your auntie take to her?' I asked.

'Oh, yes. They got on very well, but while my dad and stepmother were away my auntie had to go to Scotland. She said she was sorry I couldn't go with her, but that I was a big girl now and could be trusted to take care of myself and the home until she returned. After she'd been gone a couple of days, I began to feel sad and lonely, and it was then that I started going out with girls I worked with.

'One night the boss gave a party for his son's twenty-first birthday and I drank too much wine. On the way home, this handsome young man whom I had been dancing with stopped his car and offered a lift. We drove to my door, and when I got out he asked if I would see him again. "'P'raps", I managed to say before I went in. On the way to the office the next morning I saw him again. He asked me how I was feeling and asked to see me again and soon we were courting each other. He was so handsome, Katie. Each night after we'd been drinking and dancing, we kissed and cuddled in the back of his car, and when he told me he loved me and wanted to marry me, I was thrilled.

'Then one night, like a silly young fool and thinking this was love, I gave in to his wants. After I put my bloomers back on, I told him that when my parents and Aunty came home he would have to come and meet them and tell them we would like to get married. We made love again that same night then kissed and said good night. I never saw him again. What a silly young innocent fool I was! I never even asked where he worked or where he lived. I only knew that his name was Tony. When I found I was pregnant I was scared to tell my parents or my aunty until one night my stepmother came into my bedroom and caught me weeping. When she asked what was wrong, I broke down sobbing and . . .'

'Did she say she was gooin' to put you in the work-house?'

'No, she didn't! Why do you ask that?'

'My mum always warns me that's where she'll put me if I get in the family way. She says I'm not ter even let a boy kiss me which would lead me towards that way. That's why I'm always scared of boys.'

'Your mother's a fool! Don't she ever tell you anything about life?'

'Well, I still don't know where babbies come from.'

'They come out the same place as they go in!' she replied, smiling.

'But I was told they came out of yer navel!'

'Some do if you have to have an operation. Didn't you know that?'

'No. I was told I'd find out about these things when I got older, but I'm nearly seventeen and still don't know nothing!'

'Well, don't be fooled by what some of these factory wenches tell yer. You'll learn in time. That's why I'm telling you what happened to me.'

'Did you give birth, Ellen?'

'Yes, I did. But before that, when my stepmother asked me what was wrong and I blurted it all out, she threw her arms round me as we both wept. We didn't know that my aunty was standing in the doorway listening until she said we had to go downstairs and tell me father.

'When Aunty told him he slapped me twice across the face and told me I would have to have an abortion. But neither my stepmother nor my aunty would agree to this and so I was sent to a private home where my daughter was born. We had her christened Lillian after my mother.

'There were arguments as to who would keep her, but a few months later Aunty had a letter from a gentleman friend asking her to make her home in Canada with him, so it was arranged that she would adopt my baby and take her with her. She's now eighteen months old, and when we go over there to live, I'm told she's to call me aunty, not Mamma.'

'But do you think you'll change that and tell her the truth?'

'No, Katie! Aunty and my father said they would cut all my expenses if I breathed one word. When she is old enough to know the truth, she will be told. I'm looking forward to living in a new country with my father and stepmother, away from all this squalor, and to seeing my baby and Aunt Matilda again.'

'You're very lucky to have parents like yours. I often wish my parents would understand me, but I have vowed I'm not going to stay and live here for the rest of my life. I'm going ter better myself and I hope one day I'll be able to put all these back-alleys and this poverty behind me.'

'Well, I wish you luck. I'm pleased that you've listened to my story and I hope you've learnt from it. But remember! Always make yourself heard and never be ashamed of who you are or where you come from.'

Before she left, she promised to write to me from Canada and hoped I'd go someday for a visit. But fate had other things in store for me.

Young and foolish, I never did take Ellen's advice. Although I dated several boyfriends, I was too shy and aloof to keep a steady boyfriend for long. One Saturday evening, I was sitting alone with no one to talk to but our two cats, when I thought I would treat myself to the Lyric Picture House in Edward Street. As it was raining heavily and Mum had pawned my umbrella, I went next door and asked the neighbour to lend me hers.

'I don't lend it ter everybody but yer know I charge tuppence an' another tuppence deposit which yer get back when yer bring it back. If yer break it or lose it, yo'll 'aveta buy me another one. Don't yer dare ter open it inside the 'ouse 'cos it's seven years' bad luck!' How often had I heard this foolish superstition.

I opened the umbrella at the end of the entry only to find it had two broken spokes, but I managed to keep my hair dry. When I got halfway to the Lyric, it stopped raining and I carried it on my arm. I was early at the cinema, and as I walked down the aisle I noticed several courting couples sitting in the back seats waiting for the lights to be dimmed. As I sat down in the fifth row from the front, near the aisle where it was handy for me to get an ice cream instead of pushing past people, I noticed there were four empty seats then an elderly bald-headed man who was staring at me. I ignored him, but a few seconds later he came over. 'I 'ope yer don't mind me sittin' next ter yer?'

As I turned my head away I replied, 'Well, there are three more empty seats you can choose from!'

'That woman I was sittin' next to kept tekin' snuff, an' it was mekin' me sneeze,' he explained.

I didn't reply, but as he sat down and rested his bowler hat on his lap, I noticed he wasn't very pleasing to look at. He had a squint in his left eye and his mouth drooped discontentedly at the corners.

As I hung the umbrella on the back of the seat in front of me, he said, 'I think I know you. Didn't yer used ter werk at the Brass Works in Victoria Street in the Jewellery Quarter?'

'Yes! The film's about to start so you'll have ter be quiet or I'll move to another seat.' He sat quietly for a while with his 'billy-cock' hat resting on his lap, when halfway through the film, I felt him fidgeting. I thought maybe he wanted the men's and was waiting for the interval, when suddenly I felt his hot breath on my face and he whispered in my ear, 'If yer want ter feel, it's under me 'at.'

I shot up out of my seat, snatched hold of the umbrella and broke it over his bald head. As I ran up the aisle all the lights went on. Everyone was staring and shushing. As I reached the foyer the doorman said, 'Yer shouldn't watch it, lass, if it scares yer.'

I didn't stop to tell him otherwise, I just wanted to keep running in case the old man came after me. As soon as I reached Maggie's door I almost fell inside, but when she saw the remains of the umbrella, she yelled, 'What 'ave yer done to it?'

'Oh, Maggie, shut the door quick in case he's followed me!'

'What? Who yer talkin' about?'

When I explained, she said, 'Well, that'll teach yer not ter goo to the pictures second 'ouse. It's much too late fer a pretty wench like yo ter be on yer own late at night. Yo'll 'ave ter buy me a new umbrella seein' yo've broke mine!'

'But it already had two spokes missing!'

'Not when yo borrowed it, it dain't!' she exclaimed.

I knew it was no use arguing so I promised to buy her another if she didn't tell my mum.

The following Saturday afternoon after picking up my wages, I walked to the Bull Ring where I saw the umbrella man chatting to an old woman, trying to sell her flowers outside the open-air fish market. I bought a bunch of violets for twopence and after giving the chap one and sixpence for a nearly new umbrella, I bought a carrier bag and then some fruit off one of the barrow boys before hurrying home. Maggie was pleased with the umbrella and although I was the loser of one and six and my twopence deposit, I was glad she never told my mother.

I saw Frankie trying to stick down his unruly tuft of hair. 'Whatever is that awful smell you're rubbing on your hair?'

'It's a bit of Mum's drippin'.'

'But it's rancid. Whatever will Nellie say when she smells that on your hair?'

'She's never said anything before when I've used it.'

'Maybe she don't like to hurt yer feelings. Wash it off while I get some of my Vaseline.'

'I was looking for that, but I couldn't find it.'

'No, you wouldn't because I've hidden it away where Liza can't find it!'

As soon as he'd washed his hair and I dried it with the hessian towel, he said, 'Katie, yer know that wench yer used ter goo out with, Lizzie . . . er, something.'

'You mean Lizzie Farrell?'

'Yes. She's been 'ere earlier an' says she'll call agen at eight o'clock, but yer better not let Mum or Liza know.'

'Mum and Liza won't be back from the cinema until ten-thirty, and I know you won't split on me.'

'Well, just you be careful, Kate!'

'I will,' I answered as he closed the door.

Although I hadn't seen or heard from Lizzie for nearly twelve months, I was now looking forward to seeing her and to asking why she hadn't written. I began to tidy up the room and put the kettle on before I heard her knock at the door. When I opened it I couldn't believe my eyes. Her eyes and cheeks were heavily made up, and she looked gorgeous with her shoulder-length hair and navy blue velvet pill-box hat perched on her head. There was a red fox fur slung over her shoulder, she wore a long navy hobble skirt and high-heeled red shoes.

I noticed she hadn't changed her way of speaking though. "Ello, Katie, ain't yer gooin' ter ask me in then?'

'Yes, Lizzie, come in. It's been such a long time since I've seen you, I hardly recognised you dressed up. Come in and sit down while I make you a cuppa, then you can tell me why you never wrote.'

'I couldn't, Kate,' she replied with tears in her eyes.

'But why not?' I asked.

'Well, yo remember that day we quarrelled, when yer called me a liar, when I tried ter explain. I know I told yer lies about meself, but when I did try ter tell yer the truth yer dain't wanta listen, that's why I dain't write. Now, Katie, this is the God's truth I'm gooin' ter tell yer now. That same afternoon when I left yer, I was gooin' ter do away with meself.'

'But why? You could have told me what the trouble was? I could have understood or tried to.'

"Ow could yer! Yer wouldn't believe anyway after all the lies I told yer. But the truth was I was pregnant an' afraid ter tell anybody. When me mum found out I'd 'ad an abortion, she beat me an' put me in 'ome fer wanton wenches.'

'Where are you living now? Are you still with your mum?'

'No. Me mum's disowned me, but I ain't bothered now. I've got a job as a barmaid at the Red Lion an' a nice flat in Baker Street. It's not far from the Monkey Run where we used ter tease the chaps, remember?'

'Yes, I remember some of the fun we had when we worked together too. I missed you when you left without a word.'

'I missed yer too, but I 'eard yer'd bin out with another girl from where we werked.'

'Unfortunately I won't be seeing her again, she's gone with her parents to live in Canada.'

'Canada!' Lizzie exclaimed. 'Blimey! I bet they ain't short of a bob or two!'

'I don't know about that, but I do know they are very nice people.' I was careful not to mention Ellen's baby.

''Ow's life treatin' yer since I saw yer last?'

'Let's have another cup of tea and I'll tell you,' I replied.

I began to tell her about how I met Ellen and the interview I went to. Suddenly she burst out laughing.

'It was no laughing matter, Lizzie. I was scared stiff. I was lucky to get away when I did!'

'I wish I'd bin there, Katie. I'd 'ave got more than me knee in 'is John Willie!'

'Knowing you, yes, I believe you would!' I replied, smiling.

''Ave yer started courtin' yet, Katie?'

'No. I don't seem to be able ter find a feller I can trust. They all want the same thing – sex. Are you still going with that feller from the bakehouse?'

'No, I ain't seen 'im in months, not since the news got

out I was gooin' ter 'ave a babby. I'm gooin' with a feller regular now. 'E's one of the customers that comes in the pub where I work.'

'Are you serious this time, Lizzie?'

'I don't love 'im, Kate, if that's what yer mean, but 'e's good ter me in other ways, 'elps with the rent of the flat, an' we goo out ter theatres an' dancin' on me day off. If yer'd like ter come an meet 'im sometime, I'll leave me phone number, but yer can always find me in the Red Lion, except on me day off, Thursdays. Any'ow,' she added, ''ows that 'andsome brother of yours?'

'Which one?' I asked. 'I've got three.'

'I mean Frankie.'

'You've got no chance there, engaged to be married soon.'

'Pity, Katie. I fancy 'im,' she smiled.

Next morning I was looking out of the door when I saw our jolly old postman coming towards me.

'Hello, Katie. A letter from yer boyfriend?' he asked, handing me an envelope.

'No, Tom. It's from a girlfriend in Canada,' I replied.

'I hope it is, because I'm still waiting fer yer ter say you'll marry me, Kate,' he replied, teasing in his usual manner.

'You're the first on me list, Tom,' I replied, smiling as he walked down the entry. I often wished some of our neighbours were as cheerful as old Tom.

As soon as I went indoors, I sat down and began to read my letter. Although it was short, it was most welcome.

Dear Katie xx

First I must tell you the good news, I am
engaged to be married to a Canadian Mountie.
His name is Alan Alberto. He is tall, and so
handsome, and we hope to be married next spring.

We haven't told him yet about baby Lillian, she
still calls me Aunty Ellen, and Alan adores her.
Often it's on the tip of my tongue to tell him. I
shall surely tell them both, when she is old enough
to understand. I will write again and send you a
photograph of her, also my future husband and
family.

Thank you for the photo of you and your
handsome brother, Frankie, and I hope someday
you will come for a long visit.

All my love & good wishes, Ellen xx

I don't think she realised what a struggle it would be for
me to save. I had to give my mother almost everything I
earned, especially now that my dad had gone off without
an explanation again, though we hoped he was finding
work. Two days later I wrote back.

Dear Ellen xx

I am now putting on weight since I have taken
to wearing your corsets regularly. I have quite a
good waistline too, and I don't need them cotton
wool titties, now I have developed two real ones.
Not like yours yet, but I expect they will grow
bigger as I get older. But I have kept the cotton
wool to remind me of that Saturday you got me

ready for my interview, but when mother happened to see them at the side of the bed I thought she was going to destroy them. I told her a little white lie, that I wanted them to stuff a knitted doll I was making for my niece. I was surprised, Ellen, she believed me. I often smile when I think of that interview and wonder if he showed his John Willie to Olga, to soothe it.

I hope you and your family are well, and I look forward to your letters and all the news.

All my love and best wishes, Katie xxx

One Saturday afternoon in June, I remember it was very hot and stuffy indoors. Mum had already gone to the market to buy her fruit and vegetables. Frankie was out with his young woman and I never knew where Liza was.

As I discarded my working clothes and washed my hair, I heard distant thunder. After drying my hair I pushed up the window, and placed a brick on the ledge to hold it open. I decided to sit outside, but all the neighbours and their broods had the same idea. When I saw the old man three doors away, staring at me and waving his beer bottle for me to have a drink, I ignored him. But he was persistent and when I saw him coming towards me, I went back indoors away from the noise and gossip.

It was at that moment I thought I would change into my Sunday best and surprise Lizzie at the pub where she worked, also to see the young man she said was going to marry her. As the thunder had died away I decided to walk there.

But when I arrived, I saw several men and women sitting outside on benches drinking. The smoke and smell from inside the open door made me hesitate about going in. But I had come this far, so I picked up my courage and timidly went inside. As I looked around that smoke-filled room, several men stared at me as though they hadn't seen a young woman before.

A drunken man stumbled towards me, frightening me when he said, 'Yer lookin' fer me, luv? If y'are, yer can come an' gimme a kiss!' Just then the pot man in his shirt and a well-stained beer apron around his protruding belly came to my aid. As soon as he had pushed the old man down on his seat, he asked who I was looking for.

'I'm looking for my friend, Lizzie, who works here.'

'We ain't got no Lizzie workin' 'ere, luv. Are yer sure ye've come ter the right place?'

'Yes. She told me she worked here as a barmaid.'

'We don't 'ave any barmaids 'ere. The missus wouldn't allow it where she's concerned. Are yer sure ye've come ter the right Red Lion? Any'ow, don't yer know where she lives?' he added.

'Yes, I think so, and thank you for your trouble,' I answered.

'No trouble, miss. Yer shouldn't be seen in places like this. A pretty wench like you could get in all sorts of trouble.'

'I think I can take care of myself,' I replied, almost falling over a couple of men sitting on the step. As I walked away I heard several cheeky whistles. Ignoring them, I walked down the street thinking maybe I had got the wrong pub, but I remembered she told me she had a flat in Baker Street, so I decided to make enquiries there.

It was a small, narrow street, more like a courtyard, where each dilapidated living quarters backed on to some small shops. After enquiring at several doors, I came at last to the right one. As soon as I knocked, a slovenly fat little woman answered. When I told her who I was looking for, she replied, 'Yo'll find 'er in the room on the landin', but yer better knock afower yer goo in.'

But I didn't knock, I wanted to surprise her. As soon as I had climbed the stairs, I noticed the door was not quite closed, so I crept in. I was surprised to see such a scantily furnished room after she had told me what a wonderful flat she had. There was another room leading off which must have been her bedroom. As I was looking around I saw Lizzie come out of the bedroom almost naked. When she saw me standing there she tried to cover herself up as she shouted, 'Who's bloody well let yo in?'

'Your landlady, Lizzie. I thought to surprise you, but I can see now you've been telling lies agen.'

'Well, yer betta goo, I'll explain later.'

'Theres no need to tell me lies any more Lizzie, because I went to the Red Lion and the pot man told me he had never heard of yer!'

'Well, now yer know, yer betta leave!' she snapped.

'But surely you owe me an explanation as to why you keep lying to me?' Just as she was about to answer a man's voice called out from the other room, 'Who's that yer talkin' to, Liz?'

Before she could answer an old man entered naked to the waist, trying to fasten the buttons on his flies.

I guessed at once what they had been doing, but I wasn't going to leave until I had told her what I thought of her. 'If this is the man yer said yer was going ter get engaged to, he's old enough ter be yer bloody grandfather!'

'That's my business, now yer betta leave!' she snapped.

But I was going to have my say. 'Now I know where you get your money from for all the fancy clothes yer wear, but remember this: you've made a fool of me for the last time, and if yer ever come near me or our house again, you'll not only have the neighbours, but my mum ter contend with too!'

As I hurried down the stairs I saw the so-called landlady standing by the door. She must have been listening, for as I reached the door to let myself out, she said, 'It's nobody's business what they do as long as they pay me rent.'

I felt disgusted and angry. On my way home it began to thunder and lightning flashed, and as I hurried I got caught in the storm. But when I got home there was one smiling face to greet me, my dad, sitting in his old armchair smoking his old clay pipe. As soon as I saw him, I threw my arms round his neck and kissed his cheek.

'What was that for?' he asked as he smiled at me.

'I'm happy to see you, Dad, why did you leave us?'

'I've been looking for work. Anyway, I've only been away a couple of weeks, but there was no work about so I decided to come back home. Yer better get them wet clothes off before yer mum gets back,' he added.

I hurried up to the attic to change before he could ask me where I'd been, but I'm glad he didn't for I was never able to lie to him. I vowed there and then that whatever happened in the future I would never trust another girl to get friendly with.

True Love

I never saw Lizzie again. A few days later I heard she had left the district. I was now content with my own company for a while, but soon it was to change.

One day, when I had washed my working clothes and was pegging them on the line, I saw my eldest sister Mary coming down the yard. As soon as she came up to me I could see by the look on her face she was upset. 'Hello, Mary, how are you?'

'I want ter speak ter you indoors!' she snapped.

'Why, what have I done now?'

'Come on an' I'll tell yer, I don't want all the neighbours to hear!'

As soon as I followed her into the house she said, 'Bill was in the Red Lion when you asked about some barmaid. Was that Lizzie you've been seen with?' she asked.

'Yes, Mary,' I replied, 'but I'm not seeing her any more.'

'I should say not. If Mum and Dad get ter find out there'll be sparks flying. She ain't the sort of wench yer should be seen with anyway. I can't see why yer carn't find a nice young man instead of staying indoors weekends.'

'I ain't found one I can trust yet, Mary. Maybe Mr Right will come along one day. Until then, I'd rather be in my own company.'

'Bill and me are going to a christening party on Sunday. If yer want ter come with us there's plenty of nice fellers I can introduce yer to.'

'I'll find my own feller when the time comes.'

'All right, please yerself. Any'ow we'll call fer yer in case you change yer mind. Be ready for four o'clock if yer want ter come.'

After I sat down and thought it over, I decided to go.

There were lots of people at the christening party, men and women of all ages, but no one seemed to notice me, until I looked around and saw a young feller dressed in army uniform glancing across at me. I knew I had seen him before somewhere, but where I couldn't remember. Just then my sister came over to me.

'Kate,' she whispered, 'that young soldier keeps eyeing you. You know who it is, don't you?'

'No, Mary, I don't, but I've seen him somewhere before.'

'Bill and me know him. He lives with his sister Florrie and her young family in Sheepcote Lane. He's coming over, I'll introduce you, but I wouldn't mind a night with him meself!' she told me, smiling.

After we were introduced he bought Mary and I a

port wine, and as soon as she left us alone he told me he had often seen me coming home from work, but didn't like to approach me.

Now, I remembered. 'How could I forget? You were standing on the corner of Victoria Street, talking to a little curly-haired lad.'

'That was young Harry, my sister's lad.'

'Mary says you live with your sister Florrie and her young family.'

'Yes, my parents died when I was quite young.'

'I'm so sorry,' I said.

'That's all right, Katie, you wouldn't have known them, and I can only just remember my mum.'

We sat talking of things in general when he said, 'I'm in civvy street now and my boss has kept my job open for me while I have been away.'

'You are one of the lucky ones! My dad and brothers, Jack and Charlie, are still on the dole, an' after giving their all for King and country. There's no jobs for them now, only promises, promises, promises! And the same for millions more men.'

'You shouldn't worry your pretty young head, Katie. Things will get better, you'll see,' he told me.

'But I can't see it. We're supposed to have won the war, and now after two years there's still masses of unemployment and hardships, strikes and rioting. I'm sorry to let out at you, Charles, but it makes me mad when I'm doing a man's job, and work hard all week, I have to bring every penny home to eke out our budget. Anyway, it must be the port talking,' I said, smiling up at him. 'I'll have to be going, it's getting late.'

I looked around the room for my sister, but she had already left.

Charles smiled down at me and said, 'Will you let me see you home, in case you cause a riot, Katie?'

'Yes, after all those ports I've drunk, I might do that.' I smiled back at him. 'But,' I added, 'I'd only like you to see me part of the way, in case my mum or dad are looking out for me.'

As we walked to the end of Albert Street we promised to meet again, and he asked if he could kiss me goodnight. I gave him my cheek, but when he put his arms round me and kissed my lips gently and lingeringly, I felt I could have stayed like that for ever. It was a wonderful feeling, I'd never felt that way before. Forgetting my mother's warnings, all thoughts of that dreaded workhouse were far from my mind, and when I returned his kisses I felt I was now in love for the first time in my life.

Charlie and I had been courting about a month when he decided to take me home to meet his sister and her young family.

'You won't like the place. It's rough and there's always trouble with the neighbours,' he said one Sunday afternoon as we were making our way along Sheepcote Lane.

'It can't be any worse than where I live, Charlie,' I replied. 'I'll take you some time when me mum's in a good mood.' (I hadn't told my parents about him yet.)

When we arrived at the end of the street I saw several Georgian houses facing the high brick wall of Vincent

Street, where each door led on to a narrow cobbled street and where several nearly naked young children were playing in gutters of rainwater. At the end was another high brick wall and beyond this railway lines, where trains could be heard coming and going from Snow Hill. I remembered this district from when I was a young schoolgirl, when my brother and I took our little go-cart on the way to Broad Street, to Houghtons Butchers for Mum's pieces of meat and lights for our and our neighbours' cats.

As soon as we saw his sister on the step gossiping to a couple of neighbours, she made her way towards us. 'I can't do anything with them little buggers. It's yer fault since yer med them paper boats ter float down the drain!'

'They're doing no harm, Sis. This is my young woman I told you about. This is my sister, Kate,' he added. 'Florrie.'

'Well, yer betta come inside while I get the kettle on,' she said to me.

When I walked in, I noticed the room was almost bare, broken squares on the floor, three wooden chairs, a wooden home-made sofa and a well-scrubbed table in the centre. Everything looked clean, even the black-leaded fire irons and the grate where you could see your face, they were so highly polished. On the mantel shelf were odd vases, and beneath the shelf over the fireplace was a piece of string where clothes were airing.

She told me to sit down and I noticed she was pregnant. As we began drinking our tea, she told me her husband, Fred, worked in the tatters' yard. I told her all about my family and where we lived until her husband and Charlie came in with his three little nephews.

'He's told yer then, Charlie,' Florrie said.

'Yes, but you might have told me earlier so that I could have looked around. Come on, Kate, we'll have ter go before I lose me temper. Thanks fer nothing! I'll fetch me things later!'

I could see he was quite upset as he took my hand and led me out of the house.

'What was that all about?' I asked.

'My sister's havin' another baby and she wants my room, so I'll have ter look for lodgings. Anyway, I never intended to stay when I came out of the Army. My brother-in-law and I have never really hit it off, even before then,' he added.

'I'm sorry, Charlie. Perhaps it's for the best.'

'I'll be looking out for a place soon, but not too far away so that we can see each other.'

It was a week later when he came to tell me that he had found a room with an elderly widow, full board.

'How old is she?' I cried out, thinking I might lose him.

'No need for you to be alarmed. She's about sixty I should think, and it's a lovely house and the room is very clean, with a comfortable bed. No Keatings powder in this one, Kate. I have also told her about you, and, as soon as I've settled in, I'll take yer to meet her. It's in Bath Row, not far from where I work, and easy to get to on the tram.'

'I'm so pleased for you, Charlie. I wish I could get away from the place I live too.'

'You haven't taken me to meet your parents yet,' Charlie said.

'No, Charlie. I don't get on well with my mum. She's got a vile temper and I don't think any of my family would like me to be courting a young man yet.'

'But why not? I love you, Kate! One day I hope we get married and have lots of babies.'

'I love you too, Charlie, but I'd rather wait a bit longer before I tell 'em.'

'Very well, darling, but don't leave it too long,' he said as he took me in his arms and kissed me passionately.

One Saturday evening as we walked arm in arm to the cinema, he told me his landlady had gone away to visit her family for the weekend and left him in charge, and when he asked me to come and see his digs for the day on Sunday, I agreed.

Early Sunday morning I boarded the tram and when I arrived at Great Colmore Street, Charlie was there to meet me. He took my hand and led me to a semi-detached house with pretty white lace curtains hanging in a bay window. He put the key in the door and led me inside. I was surprised to see a well-lit hallway covered with a red-and-green patterned carpet, and the side room was furnished with cushions and antimacassars. Everywhere was carpeted, even the kitchen, which I noticed had hot and cold taps. This was the very first time I had been in such a home and I was seventeen years old.

'Oh, Charlie! What would I give to own a home like this!'

'We will, darling, believe me. In the meantime we'll have to save hard, and when we are married we'll have lots of babies.'

As he took me in his arms again and kissed me passionately, I whispered, 'I hope they'll all be as handsome as you are.'

He took off my hat and coat and hung them up in the hall and made me sit down while he put the kettle on. I was fascinated with everything I saw around me, and when he brought in two rose-painted china cups and saucers and put them on the table, I was nervous in case I broke them. As soon as he sat down and began to pour out the tea from a matching pot, I saw him place a small bottle of whisky on the table. I asked what it was for.

'We are going to celebrate my twenty-first birthday.'

'But why didn't you tell me it was your birthday? I would have brought you a present. Besides, I don't like whisky.'

'The whisky is for me, sweetheart. I've bought a bottle of port for you,' Charlie said. After we had drunk our tea, he poured himself a glass of whisky and a glass of port for me and we sat in the parlour where we played dominoes.

When we had had a snack, I began to feel drowsy after another glass of port, and when I asked what time the landlady would be back home, he replied, 'Not until midnight, love, anyway it's early yet, you haven't seen upstairs.' When he opened the bedroom door he stood back for me to enter. 'That's my bedroom. Ain't that something ter feast yer eyes on? Fit for a King.'

'It's luxurious King Charles,' I smiled, as I gazed at the bed with all its bed covers matching the flowers on the wallpaper. I felt I wanted to lie on it with my lover's arms around me. 'Why not?' I said to myself.

As I lay down and closed my eyes, I began to imagine this was all mine. I felt as if I was in heaven when he lay down beside me. I didn't even resist when he began to undress me, and we made love twice. When we had finished we lay in each other's arms and slept. I don't know how long we had lain there when I awoke and saw him go to the bathroom. It was then that I knew I had given my body willingly.

Suddenly, I thought of my mother's warning words. I jumped out of bed and as I put my clothes on I felt ashamed. I ran down the stairs, grabbing my hat and coat, and ran out into the street.

When I got home, I was glad no one was indoors to see my tears. I climbed the attic stairs and knelt down beside my bed and prayed that the good Lord would forgive me my sins and that I would not be in the family way. I then undressed and cried myself to sleep. I didn't wake up again until I heard my sister Liza ask why I was in bed so early.

'I don't feel well,' I replied.

'Well yo betta move over, yo ain't med much room fer me, 'ave yer?'

I tried to go back to sleep, but during the night she must have heard me sobbing.

Next morning when I was getting ready for work, I was scared when I saw Mum staring at me. Had I talked in my sleep? Had Liza told Mum? When she asked why

I'd been crying, I replied, 'I don't feel very well today, Mum, I think I'll take the day off.'

'Yo'll do nothing o' the kind! Just because yer dad's found 'im a job, I still need yer money!'

I couldn't forgive myself for the wicked thing I had done. When I came out of work at six o'clock that evening I saw Charles waiting for me. Feeling too ashamed to face him, I hurried away, but as he caught up with me and held me in his arms, I began to weep. He whispered, 'Kate, darling, listen to what I have to say. I'm sorry, really sorry, love. I want you to forgive me for what happened, but I love you. I couldn't control my feelings and . . .'

'It was my fault!' I interrupted. 'I should have controlled my feelings too and refused you, but now it's too late and I feel so ashamed. I should have waited until we wee married!'

The tears ran down my cheeks and he wiped my eyes with his handkerchief, as he began to plead. 'Please, darling, don't cry. I still love you and always will and I still want to marry you, so please, darling, say you will. I really truly love you.'

'I love you too, but I was looking forward to keeping myself pure and getting married in church, in white, like my sister Mary.'

'But what difference will that make? I don't care whether you're dressed in red, white or blue, or all the colours of the rainbow. Now let me wipe yer tears and let me see you smile again.'

As I forced a smile, I said, 'But it's going to be worse if I find I'm going to have a baby.'

'I don't think so, love, I was very careful not to go all

the way. If you're doubtful we'll put up the banns and get married as soon as you say yes,' Charlie answered.

'Yes, dear,' I replied. As we put our arms around each other, I said, 'And no more sex until we are married.'

But I was still doubtful. Each morning as soon as I got out of bed I would innocently feel my small flat belly to see if there was any difference.

It was time for Charlie to meet my parents. My dad took to him straight away when they started to talk about their Army life. But I became nervous and embarrassed when my mother questioned him. What was his full name? Where did he live? Was he working? How old was he? I wouldn't have put it past her to ask what he had down his trousers!

Charlie and my mother never did see eye to eye, so he seldom came to our house. Often we would arrange to meet at his lodgings or on my way home from work. One night he called and said his landlady was having visitors and, as it was pouring with rain, we decided to stay indoors. We never held hands or even sat close together when my mother was about. I'm sure she had eyes in the back of her head. As we sat at each end of the sofa, she had her back towards us, toasting a piece of bread on the end of a long wire fork by the fire. When Charlie and I began to sidle up together, she suddenly turned around and as she pointed the fork at us, with bread on the end, she yelled, 'That's close enuff!'

My periods were never regular, sometimes I would go for five weeks, but I was never six weeks overdue. I knew I was pregnant but was too afraid to tell anyone. I knew my mother was the last I would tell, so I decided to run away and find out where I could have an abortion. First I would go to my sister's home and ask if she knew of anyone, and if she would forgive me for the shame I had brought on the family. I had to confide in someone and hoped that Mary would understand my predicament and help me. As soon as I knocked on the door, she called me in. I burst out crying.

When she asked what was wrong, I blurted out, 'I think I'm going ter have a baby!'

'What!' she yelled at me. 'I carn't believe it, not you! Liza, yes! But not you, Kate! Are you sure?' she added.

'Yes, it's true, Mary, I think I must be about two months,' I whimpered.

'Does Mum know?'

'No, Mary. If Mum finds out she'll put me in a home or the workhouse.'

'Well, what do you expect me to do? Yer know yer can't hide a thing like this. Does your young man know?'

'I haven't told him yet, I was hoping you would know the name of that old lady who does the abortions.'

'No, I don't. Even if I did, you'd be risking your life and if the police found out you'd both be sent to prison! So what's it ter be? I think you had better tell me the name of your young man and where he works and I'll bring him here ter talk things over. But before I go, you've got ter tell me how yer was so foolish as ter let this happen!' I told her about the night I drank too much port and lay on his bed. 'After all the warnings I gave you ter drink only strong cups of tea and to keep yer legs crossed! Now wipe yer eyes. It's too late ter start blartin', the damage is done.'

'But please, Mary, don't tell me mum and dad,' I pleaded.

'Well, you'd both better put the banns up before they or the neighbours find out!' Mary said.

After I gave her the address and said he finished work about six o'clock, she told me to make myself a cup of tea and to stay put until she returned. As soon as she left, I began to realise how foolish I was to have told my sister everything that had happened. Would she tell my mother and the rest of the family, and why did I have the feeling Charlie wouldn't want to marry me when the news got out? Now I had to wait to hear what she had to say. It was six-thirty when she came indoors alone.

'Oh, Mary! Why couldn't he come?'

'Now don't upset yerself, just sit down and I'll explain. I waited till after six, but when I saw he wasn't among the workers leaving, I asked the doorman if he had already gone. He said the section where he was working were on overtime, but if I'd like to leave a message, he'd tell him and so . . .'

'Oh, Mary! You didn't say what for, did you?'

'No, you silly girl! He kindly gave me his notebook to write it down, so I wrote "Charlie, if you'll call at my address, Kate will be there to see you. Mary." Now,' she said, 'you had better swill your face in cold water if you don't want him ter see yer red eyes.'

'Thanks, Mary, and I'm sorry for the worry I'm causing you.'

'Well, as long as we can straighten this out, I'll be

more than pleased for all concerned,' was her reply.

As soon as Charlie knocked on the door and walked in, he cried out, 'What's the trouble, Kate? Why did you leave a message, Mary?'

'Well, Charlie!' Mary said. 'I'll come right to the point. Kate is pregnant and she says it's your baby she's carrying!'

'How long have you known?' he asked.

'I'm two months.'

'But why haven't you told me before now? I would have put up the banns straight away.'

'But, Charlie,' Mary chipped in, 'why did you let this happen?'

'We were in love and couldn't help ourselves. Now it's happened we can get married soon, without waiting. I love her, Mary, she knows that. Don't you, Kate?'

'Yes, I love you too, Charlie,' I whimpered.

'But why are you so upset?'

'I shall be ashamed to face my mother, the rest of the family, and the neighbours.'

'Bugger the neighbours. We'll be man and wife before they find out you are pregnant!'

'Oh, they'll soon find out. They always do when a young girl gets married. When the baby's born they spread the news all over the neighbourhood and then . . .'

'You just listen ter me, Kate!' Mary piped up. 'It'll be better ter wed an' face the bloody old busybodies than have yer baby born out of wedlock and it be called a bastard. Dry yer eyes and don't be foolish. He loves you, I can tell that.'

'I do, Mary, and I'll do anything to make her happy.'

'So, Kate, you leave Mum and Dad and the rest of the world to me. I promise not a word until the banns have been called and you're both happily married.'

Charlie and I thanked her, and as we hugged and kissed her she said, 'Before you go I want to let yer into a secret. As you know, Kate, I was married all in white, but I was not a virgin and when my daughter was born I told everyone she was a seven-month child. I don't think Mum knew the truth either so, if you wish, you can borrow my dress and the veil an' no one will know the difference unless you tell them.'

'Thanks, Mary,' we replied together.

'Now that matter's solved,' she concluded, 'we'll go to the George and celebrate the coming event with a drink.'

Charles and I were married in church on 25 April 1921. We lived in a furnished room where I gave birth to my first son seven months later. This was not what we had planned, yet it was the best we could do under the circumstances until things got better.

We both had plans for a better future, a house of our own in a respectable district away from this squalor, where we could raise a family to love and respect everyone, but this was not to be. When my son was a few weeks old I was pregnant again. All our hopes were dashed to the ground when Charlie was put on short time before joining thousands of others on the dole. This meant we had to look for cheaper accommodation.

We tramped for miles without any success. Either landladies didn't want parents with small children, or the rents were too high for us to afford. Our last resort was to ask my parents to let us occupy the attic, where I had slept from when I was a child until I got married. After some arguments, my mother agreed for us to pay five shillings a week including coal and paraffin, which meant I had to go out to work while my husband took care of our son.

I worked on a heavy power press which brought on my first miss. There wasn't the pill, and in my ignorance I was soon pregnant again. During those ten awful years there were two miscarriages and I gave birth to five babies where we lived and slept – in that awful attic, five in a bed. It was worse than being in prison.

On 22 April 1931, I gave birth to my last daughter. Two days later while I lay in bed breastfeeding her, my husband died. I was left a widow at the age of 28 years old with four young children (one of my sons having been killed in an accident). There was no widow's pension or social services or children's allowance in those days so I made my heart-breaking decision to relinquish my four children to Dr Barnardo's Homes, away from the squalor that surrounded us while I found work in a factory doing a man's job on a kick stamp for a woman's wage. But this didn't deter me; I worked hard and saved hard, knowing I had to be determined, whatever happened, to make a real home fit for my children to come back to me.